LIVING BEYOND FEAR

LIVING
BEYOND
FEAR

A TOOL FOR TRANSFORMATION

Jeanne Segal

NEWCASTLE PUBLISHING CO., INC.
NORTH HOLLYWOOD, CALIFORNIA
1984

FIRST EDITION

A NEWCASTLE BOOK

First printing April 1984
9   8   7   6   5   4   3   2   1
Printed in the United States of America

*To Robert Segal, husband and helpmate,
who continues to make my celebration of
life as dear to him as his own.*

Contents

Foreword

Living Beyond Fear is an important book because much of the pain and distress that people struggle with comes not from incurable inner wounds but from lack of an ongoing workable personal method for transcending the difficulties of life. Very often our attempts to understand or solve our problems lead to more complexity, confusion, and distress; and we long for immediate and dependable ways out of our binds. Jeanne Segal's latest work provides a map and a plan out of personal struggle.

Living Beyond Fear confirms my own experience involving the pursuit of core values for human change and well-being. These include the valuing of the inner self as a source of wisdom and guidance, the need for self-exploration on the path of transcendence, and the sense that it is possible to pursue growth and change by oneself, with relatively simple tools. These basic principles of humanistic psychology form the core of this powerful guide for transformation.

In addition, my experience with survivors of painful personal events, from illness to violent families, suggests that the pathway outlined here is the only way out of deep personal wounds. As the author points out, we cannot realistically move away from pain and distress before we understand its message and learn from it.

Reading this work and trying some of the exercises myself reminded me of the profound discovery I made in college when I first read Alan Watts's *The Way of Zen*. Both books describe and explore the *now* and the process of paying attention to oneself, a process that contrasts with the future-directed, hurried, anxious consciousness fostered in our culture. Both books also suggest that modern suffering has its roots in our disconnection from the essential core of ourselves. *Living Beyond Fear* is a practical guide to attain that wisdom, a contemporary interpretation of the Zen feeling. As such, it is an important antidote to the numbing that intensifies our problems and confounds our lives.

—DENNIS T. JAFFE, Ph.D.

Preface

This book is a tool for change; a hands-on tool for transformation within the context of contemporary life.

All profound transitions include rites of passage that take the initiate through the depths of fear and pain to a new level of mastery. Fear of the unknown always accompanies transformation, but the source of fear varies according to time, place, and culture. The greatest mysteries for our technologically advanced age lie not in the outer worlds of space or high technology but in the inner journey. Our passage requires us to make contact with the unacceptable and painful truths about ourselves. In facing these truths and the fears connected with them, we not only free ourselves from limiting patterns but open floodgates to consciousness of higher personal and social possibilities.

This small book contains the tools that worked to profoundly change and enrich my own life, as well as the lives of countless others. I promise it will change yours every day you use it. It's just that simple—if you will do one very important thing: Make a strong and deliberate commitment to observe and stay open to all the information you can possibly collect about yourself . . . and keep your word to do so!

With Deep Gratitude

I wish to acknowledge Janis O. Mayo, whose presence and editorial expertise made the writing of this book a joyous project; Kelley Younger, for her insightful reading of the manuscript; Donna Bass, for her sensitive editorial efforts; Riley Smith, for the love and care he has put both into the reading of this book and the design of its cover; and finally, my publisher, Al Saunders, whose integrity and belief in me I cherish.

Introduction

*If you do not get it from yourself,
where will you go for it?*
—Zenrin
The Gospel According to Zen

"Why me?"

"Why *me*?" Like a broken record I kept asking, "What's wrong with me? Why am I so angry, so depressed? Why do I feel so empty so much of the time?"

I had "made it." I was young, attractive, socially acceptable, and financially solvent. I lived surrounded by a loving husband and family in a beautiful home overlooking the sea. I had my art, my work, my freedom. I had acquired all the chocolates life could offer, but none of them filled me.

When I was active—working, painting, mothering—I felt relatively content. Activity had a way of relieving the sadness, of turning off my gnawing questions, but I could not stay occupied twenty-four hours a day. My brief forays into alcohol and marijuana were great disappointments, making me only sleepy or nauseated. I even considered suicide, but that was not the answer either. I wanted my despair—not my life—to go away.

I was reaching the end of my emotional rope, either sleeping my pain away or throwing myself into hysterical activity and worrying over my slipping façade as perfect wife, mother, superwoman. Then hope appeared. A dear friend suggested I join her as she pursued a master's degree in psychology. "Go back to school," she said. "Think about something besides yourself." I always had loved learning; perhaps in a psychological setting I would find something to help me.

While pursuing a formal, clinical psychological education, I also rushed to experience every therapeutic modality available. With a personal philosophy that "experience informs," I threw myself into Rolfing, Gestalt, bioenergetics, Reich, Adler, psychosynthesis, biofeedback, Rogers, and classical Freudian analysis. I battled with batacas; experienced Esalen; tried massage therapy and group therapy; and participated in a raft of experiential seminars and workshops. My family and friends reeled from each new "therapy of the month." I had insatiable enthusiasm. I was driven.

The potential of each new therapy buoyed me and seduced me into thinking that "this was the one," but ultimately left me flat. It also became far too clear that my teachers, counselors, and colleagues all suffered in similar ways. This indicated to me that they had not found "it" either.

Could it be that life is just hard and full of pain? Was this simply the human condition? Is unhappiness a depressing fact of life? Try as I might, I could not—and would not—accept the premise that this was all there was. I retained a very clear memory of what life had felt like when I was a child. I remembered my state of endless enthusiasm and expectancy. Joy had been a real and major part of life, along with occasional tears and disappointments. Was this something we lose simply by growing up? *Must* joy and vitality be replaced by the "responsibilities of adulthood"?

About this time, my husband, Robert, decided to enroll in a doctoral program in health psychology. Again, I was asked to join someone in the pursuit of a graduate degree, and again I accepted. The program offered a spiritual retreat; and though I never had meditated, prayed, or chanted, or considered myself a religious type, I was, as ever, extremely curious. Surprisingly, doors to spiritual awareness did open to me, and I experienced myself as part of the greater whole, much more than just body and mind. This state of awareness assuaged my fear of death and prepared me for the next major step in my transformational journey.

My doctoral project involved people who had cancer and their families. Here was tragedy so immediate and compelling that I lost my pain while caring for theirs. Counseling the dying demanded such total presence that I was able to forget myself completely. My own personal experiences with pain and despair enabled me to empathize with and support families going through their own private hell, though my agony seemed inconsequential in comparison to theirs.

After many months of counseling the dying—those who were in pain, in fear, in grief—I had a most profound insight. Those who were overwhelmed by their fear, who stonily rejected any exploration of their pain, their lives, or their dying process, usually experienced great emotional and physical torment. Conversely, those who stayed open and receptive to their deepest feelings, who were willing to experience their most dreaded fears, who spoke of and accepted their deaths as part of their lives, usually experienced a state of peace and tranquility.

These individuals were committing themselves with enormous determination in the face of the ultimate fear: death. Couldn't I find the courage to face my fear of life? They had shown me that it is possible to really change, and not in years but in months, sometimes weeks, when motivation is great enough. People fighting for their lives cannot afford to waste time or energy. There can be no partial commitment. I too decided to make a commitment. I vowed that I would face anything and everything about myself, no matter how ugly or disturbing, and become an unrelenting, uncritical observer of my fears.

Each day I set aside one hour to spend alone. I experimented with a variety of methods and techniques until I uncovered something that would evoke a powerful emotional or physical reaction. I worked with these responses, going deep into the core of them, returning to my sense of dread, my anxiety, my sadness, day after day. I guarded my time zealously, but at its end I would get up and return to my daily routine, often allowing the feelings that had surfaced to remain with me as I refocused on my usual activities.

I discovered that virtually everything I thought about myself had come from others—family, friends, teachers, idols. I knew only those things I *wanted* to know about myself, only the ''good'' things. Now I was taking a hard look at the parts I did not want to know—the imperfections, the fears, and the pain in my life that was real and tangible. I collected information about myself from sources solely within myself. I realized within a very short time that my unhappiness had nothing to do with my relationship with my husband, my parents, my family, my ''situation.'' It had nothing to do with anything but my false relationship to myself.

Hopelessness, sadness, and pain were not the problems; they were the symptoms. They were the results of my resistance to facing my fears. Now I made myself look at what I had denied all my life—the rage, the insecurity, the jealousy, the vengefulness, and the lust. I watched myself manipulate family, friends, anyone, when it made me look good, when it kept me from taking risks. I came to realize that all the parts of myself that I could never face had fear as their underlying common denominator.

The experience and inclusion of these denied parts of myself were the very source of my healing. I was strengthened and empowered. My self-created demons lost their grip on me. Each day I became less fearful. The vast resource of my energy, long held down by continuing resistance to the real me, now was released.

I experienced real love for the first time: bubbling, warm, and sweet. Whether I was fixing breakfast, making love, disciplining my children, communicating with my students and clients, or whatever, a joyousness, a feeling of profound gratitude, pervaded my life. Compassion for myself and others emerged from a heart no longer closed to life. I began to laugh even in the midst of my own pain. The more I laughed, the less seriously I took myself; the more I was able to forgive myself, the more whole I felt. I began to understand the sad irony that, as Franklin Delano Roosevelt said, "All we have to fear is fear itself." I had remained frozen in the present because of a possibility I foresaw in the future.

With the publication of my first book, *Feeling Great*, came the opportunity to do seminars, workshops, and talk shows in many parts of the country. I spoke with countless people who identified in one way or another with the same frustration, apathy, and sense of hopelessness I had felt. Many, like myself, had taken all the latest classes and seminars, read and reread innumerable self-help books, and experimented with various therapies. We all had searched for ourselves outwardly, hoping someone or something could give us the answers we so urgently sought. Instead, we found ourselves data rich but life poor.

This book, then, is a response to the question "What does it take to transform my life from the limitations of fear, stress, and depression, to an abundance of power, freedom, and love?"

PART 1

Preparing for Change

CHAPTER 1

Priming for Success

Trust in God, but tie your camel to a tree.
                    —Unknown

I always have loathed planning for a trip. Taking my attention from the fantasies of faroff places long enough to handle the mundane routines of list making and packing, stopping the mail, and cleaning out the fridge is tantamount to reading the phone book for laughs. Sometimes, in my hurry to be away, preparation was such a haphazard affair that it often sabotaged my trips. Once I shot off on a quick trip to the High Sierras armed only with tennis shoes, a windbreaker, and a light sleeping bag. I spent the day hiking with painful blisters and the night blue with cold. My friend's photos reflected the exquisite beauty and splendor of those lofty mountains. I never noticed.

In your eagerness to set off on the journey of self-discovery, the last thing you probably want to do is to take the time to read several pages of preparatory information. But I implore you to consider the points that follow before you begin. As a therapist, I especially understand the good reasons why people fail. Failure has everything to do with starting too early, expecting too much, and not taking the time to fully integrate what you have learned before moving on. So please, before you begin your hike, take your boots!

Starting with Feet on the Ground

By the very act of choosing this book, you already have taken the first step toward change, whether or not you were conscious of it at the time. This book was designed as a working tool to support and assist you in this change by making the most of your strengths and resources, as well as by providing you with new ideas and practical methods for learning about and experiencing yourself. So carry it with you, write in it, mark favorite passages—digest it and use it freely and fully.

Sacred Time and Space

One hour of uninterrupted time is the basic requirement for success with this process. This means one hour set aside for the sole purpose of being alone with yourself. If half an hour is all you can spare, go for it! But less than thirty minutes is usually not adequate for beginners. Once you have integrated the material, it will become a part of your life that you can make use of any time you have a moment or two, but this generally takes a few months of concerted effort to accomplish. During the time you have set aside to be by yourself, experiment with the quizzes and exercises. These exercises were developed to help you experience yourself fully, possibly for the first time. Your hour can include reflection, writing in a journal, or meditation, provided the activity relates to perceptions or feelings uncovered in the quizzes and exercises. It is vitally important that you find a time when you are not tired or preoccupied, and when you will not be interrupted. You may have to experiment to find the best time for yourself, but I strongly urge you to find it and keep it.

Environment is an important consideration. The place you choose should be comfortable, ventilated, and quiet enough to offer no obvious distractions. You will be surprised at the number of possibilities that exist: a favorite room, the yard, the park, a friend's home, if necessary. I know one woman who gives her children to her husband and locks herself in the bathroom for an hour a day. Though it is not necessarily the most aesthetic environment, she laughingly admits there is no phone, and in her family, "the john is inviolate." You might close the door to your office when the rest of the staff is out to lunch, or, as in the case of one very determined young woman, sit in your car. Where there is intention, there is solution!

You may find you feel less afraid when supported by the presence of a loving friend or family member, though being alone if at all possible is recommended. But if you decide you would like someone with you during your hour, please be sure that he or she is there strictly as a passive observer, so do not converse. You must understand and feel that you are doing all the work yourself, that you are in charge. Simply have your companion sit quietly, focusing on the love and care he or she feels for you.

Taking Full Advantage of Quizzes and Exercises

When it comes to making the best possible use of the time you spend doing the quizzes and exercises, there are two rules to follow: (1) *observe* your feelings (emotional and physical); and (2) do *not* judge or criticize any of them.

As would an interested but uninvolved bystander, simply watch and note your feelings: "I feel angry," "I feel very sad," "I feel _____." Note how these feelings physically manifest themselves for you, *i.e.*, where you feel them as tension or discomfort in your body. If you find yourself criticizing—"Ugh, I'll never get it right," "How stupid," or "What a jerk I am"—notice that also. Keep observing and letting go, observing and letting go. If you find you cannot let go, notice that, too.

I would like to stress that observing your behavior does not mean examining every nuance of feeling you experience. This is not to become an all-consuming, twenty-four-hour-a-day exercise in self-involvement. If, however, you confront areas in your life that cause powerful reactions physically and/or emotionally—any behavior that creates real discomfort for you—this is the place to look. Work with it during your hour, as I will explain in greater detail later on. You may also wish to deal with your reactions as they arise. The process is similar. Simply take note, acknowledge them, and go on about your business. You are learning about yourself. You may not like or even approve of what you notice, but your job is not to judge, just to do the research.

In the chapters that follow, you will find these points reiterated frequently. They are the very heart of the process of compassionate self-knowledge and cannot be emphasized enough. Until you break the pattern of self-judgment and self-criticism, until you feel yourself staying open to emotions without passing sentence, you will continue to undermine your efforts and defeat all your good intentions toward self-transformation.

Digest Rather Than Read This Book

Learning is a whole-person process, one that must engage and include memory, experience, and physical activity, as well as comprehension.

A cognitive understanding of the concepts of this book is helpful, of course, but it will not create change. However, when theory is taken to the level of action and internalized, real learning occurs. It is much like the difference between reading about the aroma, flavor, and texture of a fresh strawberry and trying one; you really cannot know what it tastes like until you actually eat one. For this reason, I have included a variety of exercises that deal directly with many of the emotions you have buried for years. These exercises will provide a vehicle through which you can begin to experience and integrate your most intense physical and emotional feelings. As this book is intended to be "eaten," not just read, the exercises are here to help you actively assimilate and integrate self-awareness. The precise way in which you do the exercises is less important than the fact that you are taking time to focus on your physical and emotional feelings.

The quizzes are included to assist you in getting in touch with the attitudes and belief systems—whether or not they are appropriate or supportive—you have accepted as personal dogma for most of your life. These are not tests. There are no right or wrong answers. There is no passing or failing. Your responses are to be viewed merely as neutral information concerning your perceptions of yourself at this time.

When taking the quizzes, give yourself permission to answer each question truthfully. Sounds preposterous, doesn't it? Why in the world wouldn't you answer them honestly? Don't forget that for many years you have been denying much of the truth about who you are in order to feel accepted and good about yourself. Answer the questions in the spirit of self-discovery and ignore the internal critic. Begin at the beginning and know yourself.

Learning about yourself—your feelings and attitudes, your belief systems, your deepest fears, and your most intense emotions—will be a process you will never want to end once you have experienced its rewards. Deliberately emphasizing attitudes and actions that support personal growth will facilitate this process immeasurably.

Discipline is an invaluable element for personal development, though it usually conjures up visions of subjugation, severity, and punishment. Quite the contrary, however; it has the same root meaning as "disciple," i.e., to comprehend, to hold, to learn. Discipline simply gives a sense of order and ease to our lives as we exchange old, inappropriate patterns for new. Without discipline, we would live lives of chaos and confusion.

"Commitment" is another word with unpleasant connotations. It reminds us of "responsibility," yet another negative word we heard ad nauseum in parental lectures. But "commitment" comes from the Latin committere, meaning to entrust, to connect; whereas the root of "responsibility" is *responsum*, to reply. Their true meanings are quite different from the implied threats of blame, obligation, and guilt we have come to associate with them. Viewed from an adult perspective, they pave the way toward personal freedom.

As you progress through the chapters, a great many sensitive areas will be stressed. If you are like most people, you will do almost anything to escape feeling emotionally unsettled or uncomfortable. But the very act of avoiding pain is the same act that dulls everything in our lives that is also useful, positive, and constructive. Remind yourself again and again and again, if necessary, that you bought this book to learn. Though some of what you may be learning is not what you expected or even like, nonetheless, it is giving you options that you did not have before. The question should not be "Does it hurt?" but rather "Does it help me to improve the quality of my life?" The discipline, responsibility, and commitment you encourage in yourself to face your fears will help you heal the very pain you dread.

In this culture, most people devote reflective time to thinking. Rarely do they observe how they feel. They examine, brood, and worry about the past and the future, seldom spending a moment in the present to reach resolution or completion. Growth, movement, and progress can take place only within the context of "this very moment."

As an experiment with what "now" feels like, try to remember the last time you sat, looked around your room, and appreciated where you were; or stood by a window looking out gratefully at the view. We read when we eat, we snap on the television out of habit, we drive with our radios on, we even keep a library in our bathrooms! We bombard ourselves with intellectual busywork and rarely, if ever, put aside a few moments to experience what "now" feels like.

If you do not believe me, try eating a meal by yourself, in quiet, concentrating on the process. Do not be surprised if it is a rather strange or uncomfortable experience. We are used to living in a world of activity and distraction, fearful of boredom and unaware of the peace we have hidden within ourselves.

During your hour return first to the quizzes in each chapter. Answer as many of the questions as you can. After completing a quiz, take time to thoughtfully review your answers. Once you have gathered the information revealed in the quizzes, move on to the exercises. Move as rapidly or as slowly as is comfortable for you. Sometimes repeating a single exercise will produce the most profound benefits. When a particular exercise starts to bore you, it is probably time to move on.

Most people will want to explore chapter by chapter, but there is no one ''right way'' to proceed. The goal here is not necessarily to complete every exercise. You will know if the pacing is correct by the immediate increase in energy that always accompanies the practice of gathering information in a context of feeling. You will have a bit more vitality each day, and your interest in other people and the world in general will grow, reflecting the changes that are taking place within you.

Some days, of course, will be more productive than others. From time to time you will undoubtedly hit an area with which you do not want to deal. When this happens, you will feel drained because you will have put effort into *not* knowing, even though you have gone through the motions of doing the quizzes and exercises. Once again your energy level, increased sensitivity, and heightened awareness will tell you that you are on target!

When you feel like abandoning the whole process or wish you had never found this book, know for sure that you are making enormous strides. The stronger the resistance, the closer you are coming to the truth. Stay with it, stay with yourself. No one ever died or went mad from the truth, only from the repression and anxiety of the constant denial of their feelings.

When all else fails, give yourself permission to stop trying so hard. Take a break. Spend a day in bed or at the beach, take a long walk in a beautiful setting. Go to a movie in the afternoon when you think you should be working, buy yourself a present, reward yourself in some creative, if not occasionally extravagant, way. Do something totally self-indulgent! Let the child in you play. Sometimes doing less in a conscious and focused way results in renewed energy, inspiration, and enthusiasm.

Above all, do not forget you have a sense of humor, even if it has been forced into dormancy. Take a step back from yourself, from your situation, from your transformational goals. Do not make change such a deadly business. Laugh at yourself occasionally. You may grow to enjoy it!

Relationships Teach Us About Ourselves—Ouch!

People with whom we have intimate relationships—parents, mates, siblings, children—help us to learn about ourselves, and this learning as it relates to our feelings is appropriate and rich material for the time we have set aside to do the quizzes and exercises. Intimates, like mirrors, reflect our own behavior, exasperating as this frequently may be. We can begin to recognize a great deal about ourselves by paying attention to our loved ones' feelings, reactions, and responses, and our reactions to them.

After listening to me drone on critically about my young daughter's self-involvement, a wise teacher once pointed out that children often reproduce their parents' past and present behaviors. This fact can be hard to accept when you have worked hard to change past behaviors of which you were not particularly proud. On the other hand, if you cannot forgive your child's behavior, then you probably have not come to terms with that aspect of yourself either.

Relationships with parents also teach us about parts of ourselves we frequently would like to disown. A fact of life we all need to acknowledge is that we inherited both genetically and emotionally. Our personalities will always contain common traits of our parents. It would be impossible for them not to. We came into this world with no real sense of who we were. We found out who we were from our parents. The attitudes, values, and protective responses we have today were primarily shaped in the first three years of our lives by our relationships with these people. It is folly to think that we have not assimilated parts of them as parts of us. This does not mean that we are our parents or that we must be controlled by ancient programming. They are merely a fractional part of the much larger whole.

It is important to note that through our responses and actions we literally have taught others how to react to us. When we go through any personal change, it will be helpful to be aware of the difficulties we are creating for others as well. They will be learning to adapt to changes in behavior that used to be predictable and, for the most part, automatic. They will be adjusting to a different you. When you stop responding to your mate, say, with the usual belligerence he or she has come to expect for some family "misdemeanor," do not be surprised by the response. I have had clients tell their mates that they began to wonder if they were still loved when they stopped being yelled at so frequently.

You also may be in the sometimes difficult position of staying open when people react to you in the old prescribed manner. Patterns take time to change. A period of adjustment is necessary for all concerned before everyone feels comfortable again. But as you grow in compassion toward and understanding of yourself, so will you grow in these capacities for others. You will keep the channels of communication open instead of building higher walls of resistance. Fear and anxiety will stop contaminating your working, social, and intimate relationships.

How Long Does It Take? How Much Do You Want?

I was told in graduate school that it takes from two to five years to make significant changes. Later, when working with patients who believed they had only months to transform, the same or greater improvements occurred within the time frame determined by their illnesses. At first I thought such swift and dramatic change was possible only in the midst of a serious crisis and only when people faced their suffering and used it to learn and grow. I still believe the latter statement, but I know now that people do not have to be in a life-threatening situation in order to make rapid progress.

About a year ago, I began to ask all my clients, including those who were not physically ill, to set aside sacred time and space as I described earlier. What I discovered was that physically well individuals willing to take the time and make the effort to fully experience themselves changed even more quickly than those who were exhausted by illness. The simple truth is that the more you put into something, the more you get out of it. This is not a twenty-one-day crash course in emotional well-being. The processes I suggest are simple and have proven to be highly effective, but they require commitment and, at times, courage. Moreover, if after you have attained your goal, you drop the process and never use it again, sooner or later you will find yourself back where you started. It will not be necessary to put aside an hour a day for the rest of your life. If you stay with the process I suggest, it will soon become habitual and you will not need to set aside time in order to practice it.

CHAPTER 2

Learning to Feel . . . Again

*We should not pretend to understand the world only
by intellect; we apprehend it just as much by feeling.*
—Carl Jung

At a recent family reunion, I was surprised and delighted—but
deeply shocked—to meet up with a cousin I had not seen since
childhood. I could barely contain my sadness as I listened to him
describe in stoic detail his bleeding ulcers and unhappy life. Was this
the same cousin who had swept the rest of us along on his exciting
adventures? Was this the same fellow who had kept us in rapt attention with his zany antics and zest for life? Where had his spirit, his
vitality, his feeling self, gone?

How Feelings Get Lost

A natural and necessary part of ''growing up'' is separating from
the dominating influence of raw feeling, such as striking out when
we do not get our way or screaming in fury when we are told, ''*No!*''
Obviously, it is necessary early in life to learn to postpone, even to
deny, gratification or to limit emotional expression. There are times
when doing or saying exactly what we wish would be totally inappropriate. In our culture, throwing food across the room when we do
not like what has been served, going to the bathroom anywhere and
anytime we please, assaulting people as the mood strikes us, are all
grounds for immediate ostracization.

Four-year-old Amy learned that she could not always say indiscrim-
inately what she pleased. During a cocktail party her parents were

hosting one evening, Amy walked into the living room and announced to her mother in her normally loud child's voice, "Mommy, my vagina burns." The room responded with a mixture of stunned silence and snickers. Her embarrassed mother whisked her off to explain a few of the unwritten rules of self-expression.

Growing up often is emotionally painful. We learn very early through parents, siblings, and relatives that others are not always in agreement with our feelings and desires. Because our safety as young children is connected to others, and since our feelings and instincts are often in direct disagreement, this socialization process is frequently frustrating and stressful.

A child's natural reaction to denied wants, pain, fear, and frustration is tears and tantrums. These responses usually are met with "Stop crying," "Knock it off," "Go to your room," "If you don't stop crying, I'm really going to give you something to cry about," a spanking, or the most devastating, the "silent treatment." Few parents feel comfortable when a child is hurt and cries, especially if they feel responsible. Their reaction is to stop the tears, the display of emotion. All we understand is that our natural responses have brought rejection. Out of our fear of continued disapproval or withdrawn affection, we learn to deny our spontaneity, repress the hurt that caused the tears, and, ultimately, separate ourselves from our feelings—just as our parents did before us.

When two-and-a-half-year-old Joey was told emphatically that he could not play in Daddy's tackle box, he began to scream and cry his displeasure. After all, Daddy was playing in it; why couldn't he? Daddy, on the other hand, felt guilty about making his son cry, so he angrily yelled, "Shut up or I'll send you to your room!" Joey had a choice—to continue to express his hurt and be exiled to his room or to swallow his feelings and stay with Daddy.

Some choice. Joey stayed, of course, but he had to do something to alleviate the stress, so he forced his feelings inward. He breathed rapidly and shallowly. He tensed his face, neck, and upper back; his diaphragm froze, his stomach knotted as his digestive system shut down from throat to anus; and he cut off the tears. Eventually, the painful feelings subsided, he breathed normally, and, due to the mercifully short attention span of children, he was distracted elsewhere. But an automatic response had been formed; Joey was learning to disconnect from his emotions in order to feel safety. He would learn to protect himself from emotional pain, but he would pay a lifelong price for that protection.

Why Feelings Stay Lost

Most of us are like Joey. We have developed habits and physical responses that have all but eliminated our capacity to relate to ourselves or others. We look at our watches to see if we are hungry or tired. We take pills to elevate or depress our moods and appetites, make us tired, wake us up, shut out the vaguest pain or ache. We go through the social motions of meeting new people but rarely make any real contact. We blink back tears even in a dark theater, chuckle uncomfortably during painfully emotional goodbyes, fake orgasms, brush off compliments, laugh nervously at unfunny jokes, avoid eye contact, and seldom say what we honestly feel. And the list goes on.

Not only do we wish to avoid uncomfortable feelings, but we live in a state of semi-consciousness during emotional highs as well. We resist being ''carried away'' by the crescendo of exquisite music or the overwhelming excitement of the vastness and beauty of nature. We are frightened off by the depth and intimacy possible in an emotional conversation with a dear friend or by the power and sensuality of sex with someone we deeply love. We negate acknowledgment for personal achievements and restrict our pleasure and excitement even in our greatest victories. Do you remember the last time you literally jumped for joy or whooped and cried in surprise and elation? We never seem to go all the way; there is always a holdback.

Stress Results from Avoiding Feeling

We have, thus far, lived our lives vis-à-vis a system of beliefs and responses that were developed from a child's perspective of life, a perspective that often viewed the world as untrustworthy and frightening. By the age of three, a child's range and intensity of emotion is fully developed. Consequently, we feel the same fear, the same vulnerability, the same stress, now as then.

Every emotion, particularly fear and anger, has an immediate and sympathetic response in the body. Our very survival as a species has depended upon it. ''Fight or flight'' is a prehistoric, nonintellectual response mechanism that kept us alive, either dashing from sabertooths or clubbing our enemies. It is an immediate, spontaneous reaction based on clearly perceived life-threatening situations. Stress, on the other hand, is not something that just happens to us; it is a psychological phenomenon we continue to create by repeatedly repressing our physical and emotional responses to changes that threaten our expectations of safety and order. Anxiety, another common but uncomfortable bodily reaction, is a result of not being in touch with our fear or of expressing it appropriately. Though the intensity and combination of these tensions vary from individual to individual, because they are usually so unpleasant, they are either deliberately misinterpreted or totally ignored. But all take their toll on the body when not expressed and resolved, whether we are three or fifty-three.

When your garage mechanic estimates your bill at $350, labor not included, you cannot release your outrage by bouncing your fist off his face (especially if he is bigger than you are). Instead, you internalize your anger, either by swallowing it and remaining coolly passive (though your insides may feel like a churning sea) or by yelling a few obscenities and storming off (which only vents rather than exhausts the anger). Neither behavior effects resolution. You may spend the rest of the day seething and then go home to verbally or physically abuse your family. You will undoubtedly spend the day reliving your anxiety as you tell and retell the story of your victimization to anyone who will listen. Somehow, though, you will succeed in suppressing your angry and resentful feelings.

But ignoring and/or repressing feeling does not make the feeling go away as we would wish. Migraine headaches, insomnia, chronic fatigue, backaches, ulcers, colitis, hypoglycemia, asthma, high blood pressure, nonspecific dermatitis, arthritis, and a host of other emotion-related physical disorders are examples of ailments brought on by repressed emotions and ignored stresses. Though these disorders in themselves are bad enough, they often are also the precursors of more devastating diseases such as cancer, stroke, or heart attack.

Emotion Is a Physical Experience

Every emotional experience has its genesis in the body. When these feelings are blocked or repressed, the emotional memories are locked in at the muscular and visceral levels.

I frequently complained to my doctor that I had a feeling in my chest as if a sack of stones were contained there. It was a heavy, constricted feeling that made me fear a potential heart attack. The tension and tightness pulled my whole shoulder girdle forward and made me appear round-shouldered and old. The doctor never could find any evidence of heart trouble.

Many months later, as I became more sensitive to bodily perceptions and began to relax and open up to my fears, I realized that I was trying to protect my heart from all the sadness I felt. As I continued to expose my defenses and denials, the ''stones'' began to disappear and my body resumed its normal posture and contour. Whenever I feel threatened, I can still feel my chest begin to tighten. But now I am able to control the once automatic response. I breathe into the tension, release it, and let it go. No more stones.

The less sensitive we become, the less whole and vital we will feel. This was dramatically demonstrated to me by a woman who sat completely motionless in my office during her sessions, immobilized by fear. Only her eyes and mouth moved after she sat down. When I asked her what she felt, ''Nothing, absolutely nothing'' was her reply, and she meant it. A forty-five-year-old male client spent years with his teeth clenched—he had not been aware of it— until an ulcer forced him into therapy.

Over and over again, I find adults mixing up intensity of feeling with loss of control. The great fear is that if we experience the full depth of our feelings, we will be overwhelmed by them. This is just not so, and for a very sound reason. While we are capable of the entire gamut of emotions from age three on, our cerebral cortex (the area of the brain that governs, among other things, judgment), is not fully developed until the late teen years. Small children can and do occasionally have tantrums that often end in exhausting crying bouts; yet, they never seem to die or go mad from overwhelmingly intense emotions. We adults, on the other hand, can choose our behavioral responses. Emotion and mind are able to function simultaneously. This has far-reaching implications. It is now possible to be both full of feeling and fully functioning at the same time. In other words, we can fully experience sadness or anger, elation or love, and continue to perform at a high level of productivity, creativity, and sensitivity to our environment.

The body is a teacher, a great storehouse of physical, emotional, and intuitive information and wisdom. Subtle but interpretable messages are sent constantly. We can use our bodies to provide the way back to rediscovering our emotions. We can relearn to feel how we feel, not just think how we feel. Any sensation, therefore, that brings attention to our physical selves is a valuable clue to our state of health, our level of tension, and our need for expression.

In the accompanying exercises, you will be experiencing a variety of physical sensations; some may feel quite foreign and a little frightening. Long-buried emotions will rise to the surface. Keep encouraging yourself at these times to give them expression. Old wounds will fade as they are given attention and allowed to heal. Continue in your determination to be an uncritical witness to yourself. No accusations. No blame. Just observation.

As you recover your innate gifts of emotion and feeling, you also will regain your natural reliance on the instinctive wisdom of your body. As you move beyond the limitations of childhood perspectives, you also will become aware of the increasing power of choice in your life. By permitting awareness of what you feel, as well as what you think, you will expand your capacity to act and to feel. You can only become more alive, more vital, more vibrant, as you regain the energy, focus, and sensitivity that is your birthright.

Quiz on Feeling

The following self-evaluation quiz will help you to evaluate your present level of physical and emotional awareness. Treat this quiz as you would a research project on yourself. Nothing is right or wrong, good or bad; all is useful information. Answer each question rapidly without giving it any thought, no matter how silly or surprising your response may be. Review your answers after finishing this chapter, and note whether or not they now reveal more to you.

Circle the answer that best describes how you feel.

1. I like touching and being touched.	T	F
2. I know when I'm about to get a cold or flu.	T	F
3. It embarrasses me to have anyone see me cry.	T	F
4. Breathing deeply makes me uncomfortable.	T	F
5. I feel "out of control" when I get emotional.	T	F
6. My feelings get hurt easily.	T	F
7. Sex is often very pleasurable for me.	T	F
8. When someone compliments me, I get embarrassed.	T	F
9. I feel edgy without a drink at social gatherings.	T	F
10. I'm able to listen when someone is angry with me.	T	F

11. There are parts of my body that are never relaxed.   T F
12. Anger does not intimidate me.   T F
13. Emotions seem to run my life.   T F
14. I feel tense much of the time.   T F
15. It is easy for me to express my feelings.   T F
16. I don't like intense feelings.   T F
17. I don't like strangers to touch me.   T F
18. I rarely get emotional.   T F
19. I pay attention to how my body feels.   T F

Fill in the letter code of the word that best applies (Never—N, Occasionally—O, Usually—U, Frequently—F, Always—A).

1. I take time to smell a flower, view a sunset, watch a scene that interests me.   __
2. I think about the past or the future most of the time.   __
3. I show affection freely.   __
4. I feel sexy.   __
5. I feel stiff and tight physically.   __
6. I feel frightened when I'm confused.   __
7. I can laugh at myself.   __
8. I would call myself a basically tense person.   __
9. I have a number of aches and pains.   __
10. I feel angry.   __
11. I eat slowly and enjoy my meals.   __
12. I love movement, dancing, etc.   __
13. My behavior expresses my real feelings.   __
14. I felt able to express my feelings when I was a child.   __
15. I'm in control of myself.   __
16. I get headaches.   __
17. I'm often fatigued.   __
18. I enjoy being playful.   __
19. I feel embarrassed when I receive compliments.   __
20. I feel sad.   __

List the five emotions that you experience most often, in descending order of their frequency.

Write down your initial response to the following questions using only one or two words.

1. When I'm angry, I feel it in my _____.
2. When I feel sad, I feel it in my _____.
3. Tension registers itself most frequently in my

   _____.

4. When I feel tense, I _____.
5. My favorite form of exercise is _____.
6. Masturbation is _____.
7. I often feel pain in my _____.
8. When my mate sees me nude, I feel _____.
9. Fear makes me feel like _____.
10. When I see someone crying, I feel _____.
11. I'm happiest when I'm _____.
12. Arguments make me feel _____.
13. I feel most out of control when I'm _____.
14. Nothing frightens me more than _____.
15. The last time I really felt vital and alive was _____.

Feeling Exercises

The following exercises are designed to help you dynamically explore many of the emotions you have suppressed over the years. As emotions and feelings surface for you, simply be aware of them without judging or criticising them. Pay attention to the physical signals your body is trying to communicate (I'm scared. I'm frustrated. I'm peaceful). Notice whether you are open to or protected from these feelings. Notice your emotions as they relate to your bodily sensations. Where do you feel stuck or defensive? Be aware of your posture, breathing, muscular tensions, or aches and pains as indicators of areas that need further exploration. When you hit upon any area that yields a strong reaction, stay with it as long as possible. But above all, be patient with and kind to yourself. The more aware you become, even when this means feeling uncomfortable, the more in charge you will feel and be in your life.*

*Italics stress the key points to recall when doing an exercise.

BREATHING LIFE INTO FEELING

Set aside thirty minutes of your hour for this exercise. Before you begin, make an agreement with yourself that you will move on to your other activities at the end of the hour. You will begin to prove to yourself that experiencing strong emotions will not keep you from your usual productivity. In fact, getting on with your life, even though feeling deeply, is the best way to free yourself of the fear you may have about intensely experiencing emotions.

Lie down or sit comfortably, and loosen restrictive clothing. *Begin by bringing your attention to your breathing. Inhale slowly, inflating both your chest and belly in any order that feels comfortable for you. Then exhale to a count of seven or eight. After ten complete breaths, continue to breathe slowly and rhythmically, visualizing your breath moving throughout the different parts of your body. Starting at the toes and moving slowly upward, inhale into each body part; as you exhale, tell each part to melt and surrender any tensions that may be housed there. Feet . . . calves . . . thighs . . . pelvis . . . lower back . . . stomach . . . internal organs . . . chest . . . lungs . . . heart . . . upper back . . . fingers . . . hands . . . lower arms . . . upper arms . . . shoulders . . . neck . . . head . . . face.* Remember to continue the slow, deep breathing as you focus on how these various parts of your body feel physically and emotionally.

As you continue this breathing exercise, it is not uncommon for intense emotions—emotions that have been stored in your musculature for a very long time—to surface. *Allow these feelings to penetrate your awareness.*

SCANNING FOR FEELING

This is a very short but highly effective exercise that will support you in your intention to stay open to your feelings. It is a miniature version of the above. *Several times during the day, quickly scan your body and locate the area that seems to house the most feeling.* Take a deep breath, focusing on the area, and as you exhale, soften around the center of the feeling. Repeat with one or two more breaths. Simply acknowledge whatever emotion that comes up for you ("Oh, that feels angry" or "I feel such joy''). Notice your happiness, too! Do not try to push any emotions away; just feel and note them.

You may wish to key into this exercise by agreeing with yourself that every time you get in your car or pick up your house keys or brush your teeth—whatever activity you think will serve as the best trigger to remind you—you will repeat the exercise.

MOVING TO MUSIC

Put on something comfortable (or, if you wish, wear nothing), clear the floor, shut the door, take the phone off the hook, and select a piece of music that moves and excites you. As the music starts, pretend you are a rock star, folk dancer, ballerina, tribal dancer, bird, chorus boy—whatever your imagination produces. Begin by moving slowly at first, until you warm up. As you feel more relaxed, move in random ways—sitting, lying down, standing, kneeling; try stretching, shuffling, jumping, kicking, hopping, spinning. Try different qualities of movement, *i.e.*, slowly (as if you were underwater), jerkily, rapidly. Try any and every type of movement you can think of to experience every part of your body and the full range of its motion. *Play with the idea of moving in as many different ways as you can.*

Repeat this exercise with one or two more music selections, if you wish, but *at the end of your last record, lie down on the floor with your eyes closed and tune into your physical and emotional sensations.* Breathe deeply as you focus on your feelings.

BLINDFOLD EXERCISE

You will need a scarf or handkerchief large enough to serve as a blindfold. Choose a room you are familiar with and comfortable in, as you are going to be exploring it sightlessly. Again, arrange not to be disturbed. Pick an area of the room where you would like to begin the exercise. You are going to begin by slowly and easily feeling your way around the room, letting your other senses expand. (See note below.)

Run your hands over familiar objects, listen to the sounds you make as you move through the room, perhaps picking up different items to examine by touch, taste, and feel. Notice how you feel emotionally and physically as you explore your environ-

ment in a much more physical way than you usually do. In what ways are your judgments and perceptions about what has become so familiar to your life different?

Now tie your blindfold in place and get to know more about your world and your feelings.

NOTE: If you feel frightened about moving around while blindfolded, you may do a variation of this exercise: Choose a table or countertop that has several familiar objects on it. Either sit or stand before it, blindfold yourself, and examine the surface of the table, the objects, etc., as above. Later, as you build more confidence, you may wish to try this exercise as originally suggested.

S–T–R–E–T–C–H

Stretching is a particularly easy, convenient, and awareness-enhancing form of physical movement that tones, invigorates, and stimulates our bodies. It also has the added benefit of causing us to breathe deeply and fully. Animals and children are our teachers here; they stretch constantly. Movement also stimulates mental processes; and stretching often, especially when you have been seated and concentrating for long periods, will enhance creativity and productivity.

So *resolve to frequently stretch and breathe deeply through-out your day.* To help yourself keep this resolution, visualize pleasurable stretching movements before you fall asleep at night and when you awaken in the morning. Simply engage three or more of your five senses—*i.e.*, sight, touch, sound, smell, and taste—as you visualize yourself stretching, breathing, yawning.

We all know instinctively how to stretch. Before and after your hour alone, take a minute or two and stretch in all directions—up, out, down, arch your back, slowly twist from side to side, reach, roll your head, anything that feels good. Notice your body respond with renewed alertness and awareness.

SOUND OFF!

Here you get to play with sound and your anxiety level in expressing it. You may feel a bit uncomfortable at first; our Western culture does little to facilitate our communicating feeling in ways other than polite conversation or an occasional "rah-rah" at a ballgame.

There are three places you may wish to try out this exercise before you feel comfortable enough to attempt it within earshot of others: in your room with the radio or stereo turned up loud enough to drown you out, driving in your car with the windows rolled up, or in the shower with the bathroom door shut. But do not be concerned. Pretty soon your friends and family will ignore your "strange" behavior.

Find your place and begin experimenting with your sounds: shout; laugh; make sounds from high in the throat, i.e., eeeeeeeh, or as deep as possible in the body, like uuggghh, wuuuff; *grunt or groan; sing; try nonsense sounds, like* mumumumumum, bobobobobobo; *make baby noises; stick your tongue out and blow a raspberry; make faces. Sound off!*

Notice how you feel physically and emotionally as you make these sounds. Anxious? Tense? Happy? Do you bellow them out or mew? Do you sound like a lusty animal or a bird whistle? Feel how much or how little you are holding back, and reflect on how that reflects itself in your life.

FREEZE

Choose three or four moments at random during the day (including once or twice during your hour alone) and freeze. Remain motionless for ten seconds. Notice your body's tensions, aches, stresses, breathing. What are you thinking about? How do you feel emotionally? *Quickly note everything, then take a deep breath, relax, and move on.*

PART 2

Opening

CHAPTER 3

Observe and Accept

But before I look out . . . let me first gaze within myself.

　　　　　　　　　　　—Rainer Maria Rilke

A woman came up to me after a seminar I had led and quietly said to me, "I would like to tell you something. I have been in physical pain for many years with a condition that doesn't seem to respond to any treatment. I have never been advised to do anything other than try to forget it or to take so many painkillers that I can barely function. Or they tell me to focus on the 'good' things in life. It always sounded like good advice—you know, think positively."

"Did thinking positively take the pain away?" I asked.

"Absolutely not," she laughed, "but it did make it less painful for others to be around me! I just wanted you to know that I tried something different today." She looked at me expectantly, as though she was ready to burst with a wondrous secret.

"Do you want to tell me about it?"

"Oh, yes!" she said excitedly. "In the exercises today I permitted myself to focus on my pain, as you suggested. I was very afraid at first, but I just made myself get into the place that hurt. It was very scary at first, though. I didn't know what to expect." She stood silently, thoughtfully.

"What happened then?" I asked softly.

"My God, you'll never imagine. For the first time in years I sat comfortably. I could put my attention on something other than trying to forget about how bad I felt." Tears filled her eyes.

"I feel radiant now, absolutely radiant," she continued, tears streaming down her face. "I feel strong, healthy—as if I could take on

25

anything—and I feel like hugging everyone,'' at which point this rather large woman scooped me up into her arms for a long and intense bear hug. In her embrace I could feel the relief and the love as it poured out of her.

I do not relate this story to suggest that by focusing on that which we dread we can change our lives forever. I imagine that a day, week, or month later this same woman awoke one morning to the pain so familiar to her and once again felt overwhelmed by it. I tell the story, instead, to make the point that the experience of observing, acknowledging, and accepting what we fear not only frees us but empowers us as well. The woman at the seminar is free not because she will never have to experience distress again but because she can respond to her discomfort actively, by choice, in a way that will enhance her dignity and self-respect.

Change contains elements that often can feel deathlike and be frightening. The choice to feel physically and emotionally is a choice toward abandoning safety for the promise of renewed vitality. It also is a commitment to letting go of our suppositions about who and what we are as we learn to observe and accept who and what we find.

We have spent a lifetime selectively amassing "truths" about who we are from family, friends, teachers, employers, and "experts." We have grown up on conditional relationships—"If you clean your room, get straight A's, graduate from college, make more money, go to bed with me, say you're sorry, love *me*, I'll love you in return." We have been protecting ourselves since infancy from the real or imagined threat of loss of love and loss of self. Though our reasons for self-protection and self-deception may seem valid and many, it is the illusion of safety that keeps us reacting in ways that are uncomfortable, inappropriate, and unproductive. Because we believe our choices are so limited and our need for safety is so great, we have been unwilling to risk change.

Researching Yourself

But change what and when and how? Before you can formulate a solution, you must first assess the situation. Since you can be reasonably assured that the problem has something to do with you, your intention to do things differently should begin with a research project on yourself—your raw materials, your attitudes, your values, and your behaviors. Only by understanding the choices you have made and continue to make can you begin to add new, more satisfying options.

Most intentions to change are predicated upon the shaky foundation of inaccurate self-knowledge. You now need to explode the self-limiting childhood myths, your less-than-objective opinions of others, the restricting stereotypic models society and the media have provided, and your own nearsighted view about who and what you are. This research project, with you as the subject, will involve learning simply to observe yourself, much like an inquiring reporter—compassionately, without the hindrance of criticism. You have been watching yourself all your life, of course, but as a judge—and a hanging judge, no doubt. You also have been watching from a perspective that most likely includes many suppositions and belief systems that may not be fully accurate. But please note: You will not continue to observe yourself if you heap judgment, blame, and guilt on top of the incoming information. When our feelings and actions are continually labeled as bad or wrong, it becomes too painful and frustrating to continue.

Do not be surprised if you find this process difficult at first. Ignoring judgment and criticism is difficult enough, but replacing them with curiosity, understanding, and humor, whenever possible, may be tantamount to gleefully submitting to root canal. Just keep at it. Soon you will begin to notice that you are taking yourself far less seriously. And the longer you stay with the process, the easier it will get.

Remaining Honest with Yourself

The rule, remember, is simply to watch and acknowledge. Observe and accept all that you perceive, all that you feel. A simple example is an exchange that occurs frequently between most couples. He (tentatively): "You seem distant. Anything wrong?" She (looking away, tense, tight-lipped): "No, nothing."

There are many variations on this same theme. Both persons know that she is lying but would rather not risk talking about "it," and that he is too afraid to risk pursuing the subject in case he is involved. So they both ignore "it."

You now can watch your own reaction patterns of unwillingness to share your feelings and consciously acknowledge them, if not yet directly to your partner, to yourself. How *do* you feel emotionally? Scared, angry, sad? How do you feel physically? Remember, your body is the great clearinghouse of physical, emotional, and intuitive information. Have you tensed your body anywhere, held your breath? Does your throat ache, is your stomach tight? Acknowledge your feelings, your reactions, but do not judge yourself wrong in the process. Just accept whatever you notice. If you feel confident enough, and if your partner is supportive, you may wish to express your feelings to him or her. Or, if all of this is too difficult for you at the time, save it for your hour alone. You may replay the scene and there, in your protected environment, go through the process of acknowledgment at that time.

When you are in a situation not directly involving another, such as getting a parking ticket, getting lost in an unfamiliar part of town, or running out of gas, again simply notice and acknowledge to yourself how you feel—angry, tense, frightened, depressed. Then get on with finding a gas station.

After you have acknowledged your feelings, thoughts, and reactions, release your focus if you can and go about your day until something else comes up that may warrant your attention. Thoughts and feelings may follow you. Just keep acknowledging them.

Noting the Positive as Well as the Negative

And do not forget to notice your positive emotions and physical feelings. What thoughts and behaviors are connected to these? Allow yourself your happiness, your joy, your elation, and let that be okay. If you have difficulty giving them a place in your life, notice that, too.

As you learn to objectively watch and assess your true feelings, wants, needs, and actions, you will recognize values and beliefs, habits and emotions, that you did not realize you had. Others you may have expected to have will seem significant by their absence. It is precisely through this blend of observation and feeling, data and emotion, that a greater level of wisdom and sensitivity emerges, one based more on fact than fantasy, more on reality than myth. You are learning how you feel.

Observation Is Not Obsession

I would like to stress the point again that watching does not mean examining every nuance of thought, behavior, or feeling. This is not to become an all-consuming self-involvement. If, however, you confront areas in your life that cause a strongly noticeable reaction physically or emotionally—any belief or behavior that creates discomfort for you—this is the place to look. If you are in a conversation with a friend and you suddenly feel like crying, or if you receive a compliment and want to crawl under a table, or if you realize you are in a rage because you cannot find your sunglasses—take note and acknowledge it, and go on about your business (or work with it during your hour). You may not like or even approve of what you notice. Just keep reminding yourself that you are not the judge in this process, you are the reporter. Your job is to learn about yourself, period.

The observing and collecting of emotional and physical information about yourself generates one very dramatic change: The choices available to you significantly multiply. Whereas before you may have felt limited, confused, and out of control, you now are able to move in new directions. Watching yourself from a nonjudgmental perspective can help you begin correcting behaviors that have limited you for a lifetime. You cut out the blaming. You stop wasting your life feeling victimized, helpless, and sorry for yourself. And as you grow in openness and understanding, you grow in confidence.

Careful Observation Leads to Change

Years ago, when I decided to take up tennis, I was dramatically introduced to the principle of uncritical observation in a lesson from Tim Gallwey, author of *Inner Tennis*. Tim taught me to focus on exactly what I was doing without making me wrong in any way. He never corrected me. He had me watch him, without telling me what he was doing. For a while he just kept hitting ball after ball. Then he asked me if I would mimic what he had been doing. As I did, I began to notice that I was moving very differently from the way he had moved, and I modified my stance, follow-through, etc. He began to hit the balls to me, and I was able to hit every one of them—even placing a few where I wanted them to go!

Tim gave me the opportunity to uncritically observe myself, to notice my old reflexive approach to tennis, and to correct my style myself, based on how it felt to do it "right." Through observing him, I was able to look at the variety of choices I had to play differently. And, *voilà!* I went from klutz to tennis player.

The experience of thoughts, feelings, and behaviors is very different from the pictures we have of them. When we do not judge, we can discern this difference. We begin to understand the underlying protections that keep us from knowing who we are. My exploration into myself produced choices. Dropping the need to criticize myself allowed me to watch dispassionately enough to investigate what these choices were. I now had the power of intention. I could change. I could test out my fears. I could stay open and explore, or close down and run. I was the one in charge of my life! This was a powerful breakthrough. I no longer had to be at the mercy of my patterns. I was no longer just a victim of ancient programming.

My behavior had not radically changed, but for the first time I could watch and not be controlled by it. I took the first quantum leap forward in my own evolution, as you will.

Observe and Accept Quiz

The following questions are intended to get you in touch with the "truths" you believe about yourself. Answer them as spontaneously as possible. Recall that all answers are valid in that they provide useful information. This is especially true of those that do not particularly please you, because they point out where work with yourself lies.

1. When my mate wants to do something without me, I _____.
2. If someone I like doesn't like me, I _____.
3. When a loved one forgets my birthday, I assume they _____.
4. When I have done something I'm ashamed of, I _____.
5. When I get what I want, I _____.
6. I don't really feel my best unless I _____.
7. When I lose control of myself, I _____.
8. I can't turn off my thoughts when _____.
9. When I'm jealous, I _____.
10. When I'm frightened, I _____.
11. When I'm depressed, I _____.
12. When I'm at a gathering of people I don't know, I usually _____.
13. When I'm in a conversation about which I know very little, I _____.

14. When I make a mistake, I _____.
15. I show love most often by _____.

WHO ARE YOU?

1. For sixty seconds, list any words that come to you that you believe describe you. Let the words flow spontaneously, without evaluating them.
2. Read over the words. Are there any recurring themes? Do any words evoke a strong reaction?
3. List the five qualities you like most about yourself.
4. List the five qualities you dislike most about yourself.
5. Put a check next to the ones for which you feel others criticize you.
6. Put a star next to the ones you feel are the most difficult for you to accept about yourself at this time.

CHAPTER 4

Criticism, Judgment, and Punishment

It is only with the heart that one can see rightly;
what is essential is invisible to the eye.
> —Antoine de Saint Exupéry

A number of years ago, I bought one of those inexpensive score-keepers that golfers use and carried it around with me for a day. Each time I had a critical or judgmental thought, I clicked the button. By the end of the day, I estimated that I had clicked off, perhaps, a couple of dozen putdowns . . . but my score was fifty-three!

The voice of judgment is indiscriminate, insular, biased, and crippling. It serves a protective cover for disowned feelings of rage, sadness, despair, and fear.

My daughter is incorrigible.

My father is cold and unfeeling.

She cares only about herself.

He thinks only about his business.

I can't do anything right.

Criticism is a voice we direct toward ourselves: I'm a bad kid, student, lover, athlete, provider, mother. I'm *always* acting like a fool, a slob; eating too much, on the make. Criticism is also a weapon we direct at others: You're *never* affectionate, happy, dependable, appreciative, here when I need you. You are *so* inconsiderate, thoughtless, unfeeling, lazy. You *should* call your mother more often, go to church, clean up the house, look more attractive, dress better, pay attention. He's/She's too fat, thin, tall, slow, emotional, sloppy, sweaty, hairy, round-shouldered, cheap, unimaginative, stupid, successful, sexy, lazy, and much too demanding.

The list is long and ludicrous but deadly realistic nonetheless. According to the voices of criticism within and without we cannot possibly ever be enough physically, emotionally, intellectually, or spiritually, and that just about covers the range of human possibility.

Judgment and criticism are no-win games, yet, to some extent, we all play just the same. It feels so natural. Our parents, our teachers, and the media modeled and assessed our values, our moral polarities of good and bad, right and wrong. "Be a good boy, Johnny." "You're such a naughty little girl, Nancy." One is as narrow and limiting as the other. It matters little what you were actually doing—you could have been clubbing your brother or tracking mud on the carpet. Every action received a moral judgment, and it did not take long before this value system was internalized. We too evaluate every possible thought, feeling, and behavior morally and simplistically, and the consequences are two-fold: Morality loses its valid life-giving connection, and anything less than all good becomes all bad. The former results in amorality, the latter in absurdity.

Judgment Is Only One Dimension

We perceive from a one-dimensional perspective when we are critical of ourselves or others, whether the criticism is verbalized or implied. Can anyone be *only* one way? Can anyone *always* be selfish, unfeeling, stingy, dumb, unattractive, judgmental? Or, using the premise that they *are*, what if they are because of conditioning, fear, or ignorance? Can we really label anyone, ourselves, in totality for something we are capable of seeing only fractionally? When we think or tell Harry that he's a dummy because he cannot balance his checkbook, and yet he is bilingual, aren't we perceiving only one attribute out of many, and that one irrationally? Whom are we kidding? Isn't Harry really just a fellow who has not learned to subtract? But what happens when Harry believes us?

We judge every situation from one point of view—namely, our own—as if it were cosmic truth. It is precisely this absolute, all-inclusive nature of criticism and judgment that distinguishes it from observation and discernment. It limits our free interactions with others and renders learning about ourselves a painfully futile exercise. We cannot learn and criticize at the same time.

When you look at yourself or another and see only one view, you have set aside rational thinking and are riding on emotion. Observation and discernment, unlike criticism and judgment, engage both rational thinking and feeling simultaneously—we can assess the situation mentally as well as feel it. We have the ability to view the whole even as the part is being seen. It is possible to see a messy room, an unsatisfactory job, carelessness, even cruelty, and dislike the situation intensely without passing judgment on the totality of the person who created it (including yourself). All-inclusive, permanent labels are unneeded and unwarranted. It is quite possible to experience the momentary coolness of a loved one, even feel the hurt, and know there remains a depth of feeling that goes beyond the immediate experience. When your mind and heart remain open, even through intense feelings, you provide a space for understanding and forgiveness to enter.

Criticism Interferes with Learning

The lack of intellectual perspective makes criticism antithetical to learning. Introducing judgment into any situation where learning and growth are sought defeats us by creating a context of tension and fear. The attitude of "good or bad" closes the door to any possibility of constructive change. Our need for immediate achievement, for mastery, makes it nearly impossible for us to achieve the desired goal; we are unwilling to be imperfect beginners. One of the reasons children have an easier time learning than do adults is that children, when unhampered by critical adults, have no preconceived ideas about what excellence is. They are uninhibited and involved in the process; they do not see themselves as awkward or inept—until someone convinces them they are. They are excited about the discovery of knowledge. The moment is magical, not the end result. Because as adults we seek perfection at each step, self-criticism and judgment inhibit us far more than any lack of ability.

Criticism of Others Masks Self-Criticism

Criticism of others is linked to criticism of ourselves. The line between what we cannot forgive in ourselves and what we are unable to forgive in others is very thin. So often the gut-wrenching responses we have toward others is an indication of disliked and disowned parts of ourselves. Those aspects of our personality that we have judged bad or incomplete, or are afraid or ashamed to recognize, are brought into focus by the unacceptable behaviors of others.

Years ago, during a seminar I was attending, I was puzzled by the intensity of my responses to one of my fellow participants. She was a bright, articulate young woman who repeatedly spoke up and made her views known. I could not find fault with what she said; but to my outwardly disguised horror, I found that every time she opened her mouth I had a terrific desire to put my fist in it. My irritation was so intense I practically had to sit on my hands.

Perceiving this reaction to be extreme, not to mention irrational, I gritted my teeth and began an inner dialogue to discover what it was about this woman that I found so abrasive. To my great embarrassment, what surfaced was jealousy. She was getting the attention I wanted, and it irked me. Here was a woman not so different from myself, standing up, speaking out, and receiving appreciation for her ideas, while I, conversely, sat in my chair still as a mouse. It was difficult for me to speak out at that time—I still had a tremendous fear of appearing ignorant or foolish. I also was extremely critical of my need for attention, for to me any kind of need was weakness, and weakness was infantile. Moreover, jealousy was petty, embarrassing, and undignified. I was trapped by my own judgments, and the tightness and pain I felt in my body attested to how much control they exercised.

Our most intensely emotional reactions to judgments and criticism can teach us a great deal about ourselves. The gut-grabbing response to someone or something can reveal in a moment what might take years to dredge up in traditional therapy. This is not to say that there are not some people and situations that we instinctively feel are detrimental to our well-being. These messages are usually very clear and should be heeded. But when we feel emotionally pummeled, we come face-to-face with something in ourselves that we are in need of opening to, not running from. Our usual response, though, out of our need to maintain our fantasies of goodness, is to transfer our annoyance to someone else. The internal critic is an indiscriminate madman who will gladly hammer away on anyone or anything (including ourselves) that threatens to remove our mask of acceptability. We can provide endless scapegoats until we finally, resolutely, are willing to expose our fraud. As we become accepting and comfortable with the parts of ourselves that we have believed are less than lovable, this emotional hammering diminishes and the critic loses control over us.

Using Shame or Guilt as Punishment

From criticism and judgment we slide easily and naturally into shame, guilt, and punishment.

The Difference Between Shame and Guilt

We feel shame when we do something over which we have no control and that act is judged "bad" or "wrong," such as wetting our pants when we were little. Guilt is a result of "wrongdoings" carried out with intent and conscious control, such as hitting our kid sister when our parents were not looking or allowing someone else to take the blame for our mistake.

How Effective Is Punishment?

Belief in punishment for wrongdoing derives from ancient dogma: "an eye for an eye." Punishment takes various forms, the most immediate association usually being physical abuse. We can punish ourselves by overeating, drinking excessively, taking drugs, or mercilessly driving ourselves with work, sports, or sex. There are also numerous ways of inflicting psychological punishment, which can leave even deeper scars. Anger or withdrawal can have profoundly devastating effects. One of the most insidious punishments is that which induces shame or guilt as punishment. As a child, a client of mine had been told that his behavior was so upsetting it had been the cause of his father's heart attack. The guilt he lived with from that time on was so enormous it literally almost destroyed him.

Webster's defines punishment as causing pain, loss, or suffering for a crime or misdeed, the implication being that a wrong can be atoned for or prevented from recurring by punishing the wrongdoer. This rationale is commonly accepted though often debated. In the long run, it does not work.

When my first child was five, he started taking loose change and other things he fancied. I gave him the usual lecture about stealing but with no effect. My anxiety increased. The next time he took something that did not belong to him, I spanked him. He responded by stealing behind my back. Not only did punishment not "civilize" him, but I felt like an ineffective bully.

The judgment/punishment cycle limits rather than extends learning. Punishment evokes anger, and we use our anger to push away the pain of guilt or shame. But some pain is often a logical consequence of inappropriate behavior. If we permit ourselves to perceive it, to fully experience it, our discomfort produces self-correction. However, this principle is operative only to the extent that we have remained open and connected to our feelings. The more we shut out feeling, the more out of sync we are with moral realities.

When I stopped making an issue out of my son's forays into others' belongings, stealing lost its thrill for him. When he was met with understanding instead of anger and punishment, he began to realize that he was hurting others and to feel badly about his behavior. Not only had my punishment of him obscured his own pain and his capacity to learn his own lessons, but it affirmed his guilt, his untrustworthiness, and his unlovability as well. I came to the realization that my need to punish him was born of my fear of being a ''bad'' mother, of producing a son who ''steals.'' We both came to trust each other again. All forms of punishment elicit anger, defensiveness, and resentment in others and in ourselves. The more we punish those we love, the more they move away from us. The more we judge, criticize, and punish ourselves, the more parts of our personalities go underground and are lost to our consciousness. Punishment is supposed to keep us safe from injury and harm. Yet, ultimately, the only thing judgment and punishment protect us from is the experience of our fears.

Now it is your turn to notice the specific patterns of judgment, criticism, and punishment you have incorporated into your life. As you observe yourself, let your feelings, as well as your thoughts, provide you with the awareness that will help free you from your restrictive patterns.

Judgment and Criticism Quiz

I recommend that you bring humor and playfulness into this quiz in order to diminish the likelihood of your becoming critical of your criticism!

Complete the following sentences using one or two words. Do not think about your answers; just let them occur spontaneously.

1. I'm much too _____.
2. I should _____.
3. If I cared about _____, I would _____.
4. I always notice how badly I _____, _____, and _____.
5. I'm not _____ enough.
6. My _____ is too _____.
7. Whenever I _____, I punish myself by _____.
8. I shouldn't _____ so often.
9. If _____ cared for me, he/she would _____.
10. I'm always disappointed with _____.
11. My _____ is not _____.
12. Compared to _____, I'm _____.
13. When I see a child being punished, I feel _____.
14. If I were more _____ and _____, I would _____.
15. When my mother punished me, she would _____.
16. I was always punished for _____ and _____.
17. The worst punishment I can think of is _____.
18. I will never learn how to _____.
19. If I were the perfect _____, then I would _____.
20. I feel punished when someone _____ me.
21. Whenever I was punished as a child, I felt _____.
22. My life would be fine if I could just _____.
23. When I cannot do something well, I _____.
24. When my father punished me, he would _____.
25. The thing I criticize others most for is _____.

Respond to the following. Again, do this rapidly, without thinking about your answers.

1. Men are _____.
2. Women are _____.
3. Old people are _____.
4. Powerful people are _____.
5. Blacks are _____.

6. Whites are _____.
7. Jews are _____.
8. Children are _____.
9. Homosexuals are _____.
10. Marriages are _____.
11. Money is _____.

How did you come to these opinions? Experience? Parents? Are you sure your opinions are still appropriate for you?

Respond to each of the following questions.

1. The ways I punish myself are by _____.
2. The ways I punish others are by _____.
3. The things I criticize most in others are _____.

Look over the lists above. Do you see any correlation between them? Any close similarities or differences? Anything you would care to change? Examine your feelings as you look over the lists.

Criticism, Judgment, and Punishment Exercises

These exercises often expose numbed anger, resentment, or sadness. Allow awareness of such feelings to surface and know that experiencing them will permit access to energy that was formerly used to block awareness.

1. *Make a list of all the putdowns you received throughout your childhood;* i.e., "You're such a slob," "You can't _____ worth a damn," "Aren't you ever going to grow up?" List all the messages you heard from parents, teachers, and other adults that made you feel insecure or inadequate. *As you list them, allow the feelings you experienced then to be felt now.* Next, *list the putdowns you hear from yourself,* the critical voice that continues to find fault with your thoughts and actions. *Are there any similarities between the two lists?* Consider how long you have been believing these opinions of yourself. Allow your reactions to be felt physically and emotionally.

2. *Have a written or imaginary dialogue with the part of you that is the "Critic." Play both the part of you that is the Critic and the part that sincerely wants to understand the need to be critical.* Begin by saying something like: "Hello, Critic. Would you please come forward so I can talk with you?" The Critic may answer, "Why would I want to talk with you, you're such a jerk?" No matter what comes up, simply say it without passing judgment. *Allow any feelings to surface with the words.* You may find yourself assuming different postures with each character. Just allow whatever arises to be aired. *Allow the conversation to continue until it finishes itself.* Then give yourself a few minutes to reflect on what has been said.

3. *Have the Critic write a letter to you.* In the letter, let it describe itself physically. *Let it tell you why it is present, how it functions, why it puts you down, if it plans to continue. Have the Critic also tell you what you can do to help, what it needs from you, how the two of you can get together to work as a team instead of being adversaries.* When you have finished, write a return letter, responding to whatever the Critic has written. This is a most illuminating exercise and an excellent way to help you integrate your critic so that it may support you, not undermine you.

4. *Repeat Exercise 3, using the Judge instead.*

5. *Think about a time in your life, probably your childhood, when you were punished.* Close your eyes and try to *re-create the scene as vividly as possible—the sights, sounds, emotions, the physical sensations you experienced.* As you continue to stay with the visualization, allow any feelings you may have to be acknowledged, whether those you felt then or the ones you are experiencing now. When you are finished, reflect on the feelings that surfaced and forgive yourself now for whatever it was that you had done then.

6. *Think about a time when you were punishing.* Close your eyes and *re-create the moment as completely as you can, especially the deep feelings you were experiencing.* Let the scene come to life in your imagination as *you allow the emotions to surface in your body.* Allow these feelings you had toward that person to be felt right now. Stay with the feelings as long as possible and acknowledge any anger, guilt, sadness, whatever. When the experience has run its course, allow yourself to forgive that person.

7. *Purchase a golf clicker* (sold at most pro shops and sporting goods stores). They are very inexpensive. *Carry it around with you for a day or two; and whenever you hear yourself criticize or judge, push the button in acknowledgment. You may wish to use the clicker whenever you feel like punishing. Use it for one or the other at a time.* This is an exercise to see just how many times you feel the necessity to criticize or punish. The very act of pushing the button, of acknowledging that you have been critical, takes the charge off your action and makes it easier to observe yourself with compassion. Eventually you will not have to use a clicker to acknowledge your feelings. Just noticing will be the "click."

CHAPTER 5

Wanting and Needing

As long as I'm trying to decide, I can't feel what I want to do.

—Hugh Prather

Irene, a strikingly beautiful woman executive in her mid-thirties, came into my office for marriage counseling with her husband, Carl, who reluctantly accompanied her. Bright and articulate, Irene listed with genuine feeling all that she wanted but was not getting from her marriage. According to Irene, Carl withheld both money and affection, did not share his thoughts and emotions, and never seemed interested in hers. Finally, she spoke of desperately wanting children, whereas Carl had no such desire, fearing the responsbilities involved.

Carl adored Irene. She was the most stimulating and exciting woman he had ever known, and he appreciated her intelligence and beauty. Despite the ongoing verbal abuse she heaped upon him, he was willing to explore his motives and, if possible, alter his behavior in order to make her happy. This process was difficult for Carl, and he struggled every step of the way. Nonetheless, he made significant strides in overcoming his fears and altering a lifelong pattern of distrust.

Carl began to support Irene in the ways she had requested. Irene became pregnant as she had wished. However, her experience of their relationship did not change. She now had all that she had said she wanted from Carl, yet she continued to find fault with him, continued to feel dissatisfied and unfulfilled.

Carl, on the other hand, though at first skeptical of his need for counseling, gained self-awareness and confidence, and no longer took part in the power struggle with Irene. Carl discovered, as many of us do, that he did not always know what he needed.

Differentiating Between Wants and Needs

As Irene and Carl's story points out, most of us are enormously confused about what we want and what we need, and the difference between the two.

Wants are culturally determined expectations that enhance life but are not responsible for sustaining it. They vary enormously from culture to culture—even from one part of town to another. They determine the roles we choose: farmer, hunter, attorney, statesman, mother, father, sheik, peddler. They stem from the value systems and examples of our parents, teachers, friends: I want to look like, act like, feel like, Marilyn Monroe, John Wayne, Wonderwoman, Ghandi, The Beatles, my best friend, my Latin teacher; I want to have a sports car, a fur coat, a faster motorboat, a bigger ranch with more cattle, a $200,000-a-year salary, more hair, less fat, a house at the beach, security, popularity. Beliefs formulated in childhood about wants and dislikes continue to play a large part in what we want and, therefore, in what we choose to pursue.

Belief systems also still determine our friendships, our romantic relationships, our general views about whom we like and do not like. For example, a woman who has had more supportive female role models than male role models will understandably expect more dependability, sensitivity, etc., from women; and the relationships she has with men will be colored by the beliefs she has formulated about them, *i.e.*, men are aggressive, inconsiderate, untrustworthy, and so on.

Often in a complex culture like ours we get confusing or mixed messages about what to want. "Have a good time," but "never lose control." "Money isn't everything," but "cheat on your income tax if you can get away with it." "Look sexy," but "don't have sex." Parents tell us one thing, friends another; teachers, heroes, the media, tell us something else again. Confusing? You bet.

A need, on the other hand, is something a person cannot do without. It maintains and sustains life. Needs ignore cultural and social boundaries. All people share in their dependence upon a relatively few basic necessities. Some needs, however, are more commonly acknowledged and understood than others. Most people readily accept their physical needs for sufficient food and protection from the elements. Psychological and spiritual needs, though, often go unseen and unmet: the need to love and to be valued, the need to contribute to life, the need to experience ourselves beyond our physical dimensions. These, too, are basic needs. But we have been taught either to ignore these needs, to hate the dependency that needs impose, or to believe in the futility of ever satisfying them.

Life itself often is the tragic price we pay by choosing to deny what we must have. Obviously, we will die faster from lack of water than from lack of emotional security or spiritual connectedness. But lacking any basic needs, we eventually lose hope and the will to continue, which initiates a degenerative process.

The precise ways we meet our needs vary from individual to individual, though the needs themselves do not. The need for good health can be met by eating a variety of foods that supply basic nutritional requirements. The need for recognition and appreciation may or may not be met by a hug, a promotion, a present, a kind word, an M & M, or a gold watch, but somehow this need for self-worth must be fulfilled; and because we are social creatures, we need the support and occasional succor of others. Babies do not fully develop intellectually, physically, or psychologically unless they receive loving physical attention. They may even die if deprived of it. Food and shelter alone are not enough to sustain life.

What we need is far more necessary than what we want in order to maintain a healthy and vital life. The fact is that, like Irene, most of us do not know the difference between a want and a need, so how can we begin to decide what it is we really want, much less really need? Some of us are so closed down that we cannot differentiate between what is life-sustaining and what is not.

Why? Because we tend, especially as adults, to determine both our wants and needs intellectually, without consulting our physical and emotional selves. Consequently, we often pursue our wants and needs on the basis of other peoples' values and belief systems learned in childhood. Instead of asking, "What do I need in order to feel well?" or "What do I want that feels synchronous with my values?" and heeding the life-sustaining information conveyed, we ask anxiously, "What should I want?" "What do they want?" and/or "What can I get that will impress others?" We abandon our feeling selves to our thinking but often confused selves.

There is a popular questionnaire that asks people to list the ten activities they most often enjoy doing, and then to consider how recently and often they do them. Most people discover they seldom do the things they feel like doing. Many people, in fact, believe they should feel guilty if they enjoy what they are doing. As a friend sadly says, ''If I enjoy doing it, then it must be fattening, illegal, or immoral.'' What we fail to take into consideration is that by consistently ignoring our needs and doing what we do not want to do, we are slowly (or perhaps rapidly) undermining our health and well-being.

Feelings Clarify Wants and Needs

Tuning in to our needs brings into focus the deeper value of our actions and helps us better distinguish between what we want and what we need. My twelve-year-old daughter told me one day that she had cheated at school but had discovered that she felt terrible afterward. She thought that what she really had wanted was an easy A; but because she was in tune with her feelings, she found she had lost something of greater value in the process—her self-respect.

Puberty is a time when we all come to grips with conflicting wants. It is a time when we are particularly vulnerable as we strain to prove our individuality, to attain autonomy. Yet even during the fragile adolescent years, those who learn from their feelings move ahead, whereas those who ignore feelings lose touch with themselves and are destined to repeat their inappropriate and unsuccessful behaviors.

It may have seemed that death was imminent when we were thirteen or fourteen and were not chosen to be on the team or asked to the party by Handsome Hunk or elected to school office; but we survived. If somehow we managed to stay open to what we were feeling, we probably also noticed that the pain of losing or of feeling rejected or discounted diminished when we pursued other activities that made us feel good about ourselves. Sadly, few of us seem to remember this.

Teenagers do not have the exclusive rights to confusion about conflicting wants and needs. As adults we still seek honors and love, popularity and self-esteem. But honors and popularity are wants; love and self-esteem are needs. The rule of thumb may be expressed as: If what you want will deeply affect your life emotionally, physically, or psychologically, then it is a need; everything else is a want.

These distinctions are illumined by what we feel. By ignoring our feelings, we can fool ourselves for a while into believing we are getting what we really need. Irene's husband, Carl, did so by telling himself he did not need caring for. Shut off from most of his emotions, he believed he was satisfied with his relationship with Irene.

By insisting that her incessant nagging and criticism of him did not matter a bit, he sold himself a bill of goods. That he loved her was not the issue; that he had convinced himself that it did not matter to him that she was not loving toward him, though, was his sad attempt to stay disconnected from the pain of a denied need. This behavior eventually wore him down.

Early in Carl's life, his child's mind had decided that it hurt too much to long for the nurturing that rarely materialized, so he chose instead to cut himself off from those feelings. As he grew older, he began to assume the posture that he did not need anything from anyone; still not dealing with the pain, he often became depressed in order to survive the discomfort. But once he began to perceive his real feelings, all this dramatically changed. He realized how deeply hurt and angry he was that his life contained so little caring and affection from others.

Irene also had disconnected early in her life from her needs for self-esteem and love, both in giving and receiving. Somewhere along the line, she had decided that others should take responsibility for her well-being. When she finally discovered that others could not satisfy her needs even if they wanted to, as Carl did, she was forced by her own unhappiness to accept responsibility for her feelings.

Focusing on our physical and emotional feelings, including those that are, at times, painful, can prove invaluable in directing us toward our true needs and attitudes. Knowing what we need and accommodating our wants accordingly enables us to use our energies appropriately and economically so that we avoid the pursuit of goals that are deleterious to us. Being in touch with what we truly need enables us to use our resources fully and in ways that will ensure a lifetime of health, well-being, and fulfillment.

Now it is again your turn to devote yourself to your research project, this time aimed at clarifying the relationship between the wants and needs in your life. Begin to ask yourself the following questions: What are my true needs? How important to me are the things that I want compared to the things that I need? Do the things that I want support or conflict with my needs? Am I protecting myself from the frustration or sadness of acknowledging a need that I believe cannot be met? The more emotional you become as you tackle this project, the more you will get out of it. It may even save your life!

Wants and Needs Quiz

Without thinking about each entry, circle the items on the list that strike you as something you cannot live without. Do not let your judgment or criticism interfere with your honesty.

Cigarettes	A spouse
Love	Therapy
A new car	A family
Good health	Vacations
Self-respect	Time for yourself
Food	Tension
Popularity	A sense of purpose
Children	Luxury
A satisfying sex life	Beauty
Financial security	A housekeeper
Fame	Music
Job satisfaction	Laughter
A beautiful house	Outdoors experiences
Comfort	A spiritual life
Drugs	Money
A television set	A tan
Nurturing	Fashionable clothing
A job	Friends
Self-expression	A secretary
Pets	Sports
Water	A lover
Fear	Self-control
Esteem of others	Intimacy
Hobbies	A personal value system
A home	Credit cards
New ideas/learning	Emotional support

This is by no means a complete list. Please feel free to add your own items to the ones above.

To get in touch with what you believe are the differences between your wants and needs, fill in each blank with either the word "want" or "need." Do not stop to consider your choice. Once you have completed the quiz, review your answers as might a dispassionate observer. Do some of your choices surprise you?

1. I _____ to be first.
2. I _____ to be approved of.
3. I _____ to be the center of attention.
4. I _____ to look good.
5. I _____ to dress fashionably.
6. I _____ to be in control at all times.
7. I _____ money to live well.
8. I _____ to take care of my body.
9. I _____ to enjoy myself.
10. I _____ to feel well.
11. I _____ to share my true feelings.
12. I _____ to laugh and play.
13. I _____ to feel good about myself.
14. I _____ to have a nice car.
15. I _____ to be creative.
16. I _____ friends.
17. I _____ nurturing food.
18. I _____ a satisfying job.
19. I _____ a loving relationship.
20. I _____ opportunities for self-expression.
21. I _____ junk food.
22. I _____ to feel safe and protected.

Wants and Needs Exercises

Remember to consult your physical and emotional feelings for the most factual information in the exercises that follow.

1. Spend a few minutes reflecting on the things you believe you *need* to live long and well, focusing on your feelings as well as on your thoughts. Then *list ten things that you feel are indispensable to your continued well-being.*

2. Place a check by the needs you listed above that you feel are not being met at this time.

3. List the ten things you most *want*. Write down anything that you would like to have, no matter how silly or extravagant it may seem.

4. Put a check next to the wants listed above that you feel you deserve. How many items did you feel you deserve? All of them? Some of them? Compare how deserving you feel with how difficult you think your wants are to obtain.

5. *Compare the above two lists of needs and wants.* Are there any similarities? Any obvious differences? On another sheet of paper, *put your lists in descending order of importance.* Are there any significant changes from their original order? How do you feel about what you have observed?

6. *Spend one entire day paying attention to how many times you hear yourself say, "I want" or "I need," whether aloud or to yourself.* Notice which one you hear most frequently. Notice what you want and need most frequently.

7. On a piece of paper, *list the ten things you most want to do.* On the same piece of paper, *list the ten things you most often do.* Compare the two lists. Are they the same? Different? What do you feel about the differences? What would you like to change?

CHAPTER 6

Learning to Live with Fear

What you are afraid of overtakes you.
                    —Estonian proverb

In Sartre's *No Exit*, three people are trapped in a metaphor of personal hell: a bizarre, mirrorless room with locked doors. After they have agonized and argued over their torturous plight, a door suddenly opens—a way into freedom and the unknown. They are free to go but choose, instead, to remain in their now self-imposed cell.

We too may choose freedom; but do we? We can reach out for loving relationships, close friendships, the warmth and nurturing that only other human beings can provide; but do we? We can reflect, take time for ourselves, relax, enjoy life and the opportunities it presents; but do we? As researchers of ourselves, we have begun uncovering the knee-jerk responses that clearly diminish the quality of our lives. We can stop responding in ways that block our intentions, our needs, our creativity, our joyousness; but will we? Or will we continue to choose a prison without doors?

Reflexive Responses Trigger Pain and Loss

We have been unaccepting of our natural feelings and emotions for a long, long time. They were the source of fear and loss of love when we were young, and they remain deeply buried. We all have buttons that when pressed elicit feelings and responses whose origins and mechanics we are at a loss to explain. The discomfort produced today, though, is no less intense or uncomfortable than it was when we were small.

Johnny, two-and-a-half, rides his tricycle with blissful abandon. His mother sits in the yard, watching him pedal happily up and down the sidewalk in front of their home. Her next-door neighbor appears and asks to borrow a cup of flour. Thinking she will be only a moment, she tells Johnny imperatively to "stay on the sidewalk," and goes inside with her neighbor to get the flour. The phone rings and she answers it. Meanwhile, Johnny is thrilled to discover that if he pedals up to the crest of the driveway, he can rocket down the other side, stopping just short of the street. He does this gleefully a couple of times and has topped the crest once more as his mother and her friend reappear. She gasps as she sees him and screams, "Johnny, *no!*" just as he begins his downward roll. Startled, he jumps, his feet fall off the pedals, and he rolls out into the middle of the street. He hears the screech of brakes as his tricycle overturns. Moments later, obviously not seriously hurt but scraped and stunned, he is jerked up and smacked repeatedly on the behind as his mother hysterically rebukes him for riding in the street and sends him to his room under a barrage of disapproval. He is confused, embarrassed, and frightened by his mother's behavior. He also is still reeling from the terrifying sight and sound of a car stopping inches away from him.

Today, at forty, John continues to react to anger in the same way. When another person becomes angry and raises his/her voice at him, he feels powerless and paralyzed, then withdraws. He closes down on his own feelings of anger and resentment, and leaves the room. John does not really know why he reacts this way. He simply does.

No one negative experience is the basis for our lifelong protective patterns, of course. As was discussed earlier, these reactions are a product of the quality of care and love we felt from the significant people in our lives, primarily from our parents. Our reflexive responses to pain and loss were established long ago in childhood. Most of these responses are inappropriate and unnecessary now that we are adults. Nonetheless, we feel we are not as good, nice, unselfish, or lovable as we would like or expect to be. We try again and again to act differently, more appropriately, but repeatedly get caught in emotions that trigger these unproductive patterns. As a result, we often feel helpless to effect real change.

It requires a great deal more to change our behavior than just the desire to do so. We all are basically willing to accept personal transformation—but only if it is harmless, painless, and easy. Yet permanent change in never easy. Experiencing ourselves deeply is difficult, frightening, and can be emotional painful. Down in some deeply buried vault of our being lies the dread that if we allow ourselves to fully experience the emotions we so carefully deny, we will be over-whelmed by their power and lose our "selves" forever.

Facing Fear While You Are Fearful

Fear keeps us imprisoned, even when the doors are wide open and we have known routes of escape. To overcome fear, to control it in-stead of allowing it to control us, we must choose to meet the chal-lenge of fear itself. But there is only one way out: We must take the first step forward while we are still afraid. In order to move ahead, we must experience the very things of which we are most fearful.

Had John spent ten years in traditional therapy to finally uncover, in a moment of triumphant illumination, that he reacts the way he does primarily because of numerous incidents like the tricycle trauma, his established patterns of anger/withdrawal still would not have suddenly disappeared. He would have had an insight into the "why" of his reactive behavior; and gathering enough insights, he may have formed some basic concepts about his avoidance of pain. But chances are he still would be removing himself from his emotions by repeatedly intellectualizing his feelings rather than feeling them. This distancing from emotions is the primary reason most people do not change even when they "know better."

Reasons are necessary to the extent that they explain the motivating forces behind our outdated needs for protection, but they are not justifications. They supply information, not transformation. Their real value lies in opening us to understanding and, inevitably, compassion. It becomes progressively easier for us to watch our pat-terns in the light of forgiveness than to do so beneath a veil of self-criticism and blame. Fear has been at the root of all our negative responses. It is much less threatening to react symptomatically with anger, depression, withdrawal, or punishment than it is to ex-perience fear itself.

Feeling the Fear

You are now reaching a point in the process of self-exploration where the going gets tougher. The difference between mentally pro-cessing a feeling and experiencing that feeling is vast and often terri-fying. The real solution lies in our capacity to fully experience the very emotions from which we have been protecting ourselves. It is through this raw experience of feeling what we most want to avoid that we gain resolution and, ultimately, freedom.

Let's take a look at some of our fears. From what *do* we protect ourselves? Of what are we afraid? Here is a list of the most common fears I have observed, but feel free to add your own to it.

1. We fear the loss of love.
2. We fear the loss of purpose and meaning in our lives.
3. We fear physical degeneration, disease, loss of energy.
4. We fear pain.
5. We fear the loss of our loved ones.
6. We fear the loss of status, job, material possessions, especially if we believe that our identity is attached to these things.
7. We fear being wrong, looking foolish, being ignorant.
8. We fear the loss of control, the possibility of insanity.
9. We fear death.
10. We fear the unknown, the untried.
11. We fear life, its unpredictability and responsibility.

Though we all experience some degree of fear of all the items on the list, a few will undoubtedly elicit deeper or more powerful responses. Any one of them offers us a place to begin our process of self-exploration. If we look into the areas we want most to avoid, we will discover what frightens us most.

Were John to open up to his feelings, he would be impacted by the terror lying below his seething anger. What he would experience most profoundly would be his fear of abandonment, his fear of disapproval and loss of love. He also would become painfully aware that he is afraid to love others. As a child, he frequently was yelled at for his natural curiosity and behavior. The singular example of the tricycle was typical of his childhood—he often was surprised and frightened by his mother's anger, and exiled to his room. At that tender age, however, he had no way of explaining, much less understanding, his mother's behavior—her fears for his safety, her embarrassment in front of others, her need to maintain ''control'' of her child, her guilt-produced rages. Instead, he doubted and distrusted himself, his perceptions, his feelings. Today he continues to doubt and distrust both himself and others.

Emotions connected to past experiences and belief systems that no longer work for us often play dominant roles in our present lives. An extreme but particularly powerful example of this is evident in the story of Laura, a young woman battling for her survival.

Laura came to me two years ago, desperate and terrified. She was suffering from bulimia, an emotional compulsive-eating disorder. The bulimic devotes considerable time and effort to planning, buying, and preparing the food for his/her binges; eats beyond capacity; and finally wretches and vomits, then repeats the cycle until he/she is spent, both physically and emotionally. Through traditonal psychological methods, treatment is lengthy, if at all successful. Bulimia is an elaborate and powerful escape—and Laura had been repeating some form of this behavior since the age of eight. She was then nearly thirty.

Laura worked very hard to experience her feelings before, during, and after her binges. She spoke of great wrenching pain, shooting from the bottoms of her feet through her chest and heart and culminating at the top of her head. She was filled with intense self-loathing. What she discovered beneath her self-hatred was despair that she had been an enormous disappointment to her parents, that she had failed to meet any of their expectations in any way. She wished she would die and hoped that she would be found in a pool of vomit, that she would disgrace her parents and make them profoundly sorry for having pressured her as they had.

Now, at last, Laura has given her deepest emotional and physical feelings permission to surface, to enter the very marrow of her fear and despair. She is beginning to recognize her own self-worth and eagerly continues in her self-discoveries. For the first time in her life, Laura has begun to have nurturing and fulfilling relationships. She also has come to understand that her belief in her parents' disapproval and disappointment had been conceived by a child of four or five, and did not necessarily reflect "the truth" as she had been interpreting it.

Laura is reversing a lifelong pattern, as you are. Instead of pushing fear away through her protective reactions, she has opened herself to her deepest feelings, including fear. To her surprise, she neither died nor went crazy but found, instead, the strength and power within herself to continue. Finally she has taken control of her life.

Blending Intellect with Emotion

The process of appropriately experiencing intensely difficult feelings integrates three of the most significant aspects of our personality—the frightened child, the loving parent, and the rational adult. It is a blending of our raw emotions, compassionate self-awareness, and innate intelligence and wisdom that produces quantum leaps toward self-mastery, choice, and freedom. It requires self-discipline—moments when we have to "tough it," when we would rather indulge ourselves in self-pity and blame. Often it will appear to be a halting process when, seemingly overnight, we will make great strides forward. At other times, we may feel as though we were quagmired in a morass of inertia. But something strange and exciting is taking place all the while. Throughout this process, barely noticeable at first, we will begin to accept our own beauty and intrinsic worth. We will stay open even in pain or conflict. Our desire for personal exploration and growth will move us beyond our pain and fear. Choice is power and power is freedom, and choice ultimately will set us free.

CHAPTER 7

Ride the Wild Horse

*All of us collect fortunes when we are children—a
fortune of colors, of lights and darkness, of movements, of tensions. Some of us have the fantastic
chance to go back to our fortune when we grow up.*
                                              —Ingmar Bergman

The format of the following detailed exercise is one I recommend
throughout this book. It is the essential experience from which the
exercises that follow are drawn. Read through it carefully before
beginning. (Beginner and advanced versions of this exercise are
available on tape at your bookseller.)

Once again, I urge you to ignore the voice of criticism, the
judgmental mind, as it tries its best to undermine your efforts to experience your feelings. Go gently and compassionately as you set out
on your journey into feeling and wholeness.

Preparation

Prepare for this experience by creating as safe and comfortable an
environment as you possibly can. The following points should help
you make the most of your time and energy:

- Take off your shoes and loosen your clothing.
- Take the phone off the hook, lock the door if necessary. You
  might even wish to hang a *Do Not Disturb* sign on the door.
- Select a chair or bed you find most comfortable. Some people
  prefer lying on a carpeted floor.

- Set a timer or alarm if you think you will be watching the clock. Sixty minutes is ideal, but less than thirty minutes is inadequate. This is a time-limited exercise. Giving yourself too little time can make you feel tense and distracted, whereas too much time can result in your not fully applying yourself.
- Stretch and move around before and after the exercise. And do not forget to move and exercise several times a day. Movement is especially helpful in releasing the muscular discomfort that often accompanies intense feelings.
- Please do not smoke, drink, or use any drugs (except those your doctor has specifically prescribed) before or during the session. Please do not eat a large meal just before your hour; it probably will make you sleepy. And, of course, do not eat during the hour.

Instructions

Begin by clearing your mind of all thoughts. Take several slow, deep breaths, releasing your thoughts with each exhalation. As you continue, allow your body to sink comfortably into the chair, bed, or floor.

Recall a recent experience in which you reacted with inappropriate intensity. Perhaps you experienced significant physical/emotional discomfort in some unthreatening situation or for no apparent reason. Re-create this moment as vividly as you can. Touch, taste, and smell the situation as well as hear and see it in your mind's eye. As you continue breathing as fully and deeply as is comfortable for you, begin scanning your body (refer to Chapter 2, page 19) for any part that holds the most intense feeling. Do not be concerned if you find tension where you least expected it; once you locate it, direct your full attention toward it and breathe into its center.

Your attention undoubtedly will wander away frequently to unrelated thoughts and images. Each time this happens, gently bring it back with your breath and refocus on the physical/emotional feelings stored in the body part.

Permitting All That's There to Surface

Continue breathing deeply, allowing the intensity to grow. Permit yourself to be frightened, angry, or sad, if that is how you feel. You may find it helpful to add the thought or verbal command "Permit the feeling" or "Allow the feeling" as you inhale and exhale.

If you begin with one emotion but find that it shifts or dissolves into another, or if the source of the feeling moves to another area of the body, permit this to happen. Continue to focus on each new feeling exactly as you did its predecessor, allowing it to be experienced fully, allowing it to intensify. Feelings can transform in an instant; rage can become sadness, sadness can give way to pain, grief can dissolve into rage. Any and all can transform into fear. Follow the feeling wherever it goes. An image that I especially like is that of riding a wild horse. Your feeling, like the bucking, rearing horse, is full of fear and unbridled energy. The only way to tame it is to stay with it, to prove to it that it will not be hurt and that you will not be thrown off.

Once a feeling has intensified, stay with it for ten to twenty minutes. Afterward, you may further get in touch with your feelings by directing questions to the feeling source in your body, *not your mind.*

- Are you a new feeling?
- If not, when did I first feel you?
- Do I feel you often?
- What do you have to teach me about myself?
- What is the feeling I am experiencing? Is it rage? Sadness? Fear? Is it the despair of numbing?

If an answer does not surface, do not be concerned. It is far more important to feel your feelings than to categorize them. You may wish to deepen your understanding by continuing to ask questions: "If I'm sad, why am I sad, and why does that make me sad?" "If I'm angry, why am I angry, and why does that make me angry?" This kind of uncritical, gentle probing eventually will reveal hidden fear. Typically, we are most afraid of what could be or of what might happen related to the limited impressions and understanding we had as children.

Questions like these can elicit intuitive responses that reveal in a moment what you may have missed recognizing for years. Sometimes a very strong release of emotional energy is experienced. Tears may flow; you may groan, cry out, speak, or wail. This is an indication that you have indeed broken through an area of blocked emotional energy. If, as you approach an intense feeling, you go numb, let the feeling of non-feeling become your focus. (You may wish to refer to Chapter 10.) Keep in mind that it is perfectly okay to feel frightened. The feeling of fear will never kill you or cause you to go mad because you have the intellectual capacity to direct your emotions appropriately.

Progress, however, often is less dramatic, though no less effective; it may take place over hours, even days. The analogy here is that of a slow-draining wound. The more that is released, the better you feel. This exercise is designed to initiate the opening of the block, and stored energy will continue to be released until you feel comfortable, equalized, and positively energized.

Holding the Feeling But Not the Thought

Ending is one of the most important parts of this exercise. When your time is up, stop focusing on the feelings with your mind but continue experiencing them physically and emotionally. I repeat, *stop thinking about the feelings.* It is vital for you to learn that you can feel intensely and direct your thoughts to other matters—your work, your family, and so on. Your feelings may be childlike, but you have the developed intellect of an adult to deal with them.

Obviously, if you do the exercise just before you go to sleep, you will not be able to continue your daytime activities. Because of the importance of experiencing your routine while you are fully conscious of your feelings, I do advise doing the exercise before bedtime.

When your time is up, pause for two or three minutes, breathing slowly and rhythmically, and relaxing. You will notice your mind busying itself again. After this pause, get up and go about your day but allow the physical/emotional feelings you have uncovered to remain with you.

To summarize:

- *Create an environment of comfort and safety.*
- *Clear your mind and concentrate on breathing fully and deeply.*
- *Recall a recent experience in which you reacted with inappropriate intensity. Scan your body and observe which part houses the most feeling when you recall this experience.*
- *Focus fully on this area and direct your breath to it.*
- *Ride the experience for ten to twenty minutes.*
- *Deepen with questions, which will reveal the source of the feeling.*
- *End the exercise by continuing to feel the feelings that have emerged, but direct your thoughts and attention elsewhere.*

The more you work with this process, the less time you will need to locate and intensify your feelings and the more comfortable you will grow in allowing yourself to experience them. Eventually, you will be confident enough to permit intense feelings to be experienced fully at any time, and secure in the knowledge that you can appropriately experience and direct them.

The intensity that may be evoked while doing this exercise is the result of tapping into emotions and energies that may have been trapped, unable to be released, for many years. A current problem may have triggered them; but like the tip of the iceberg, most of the mass remains below the surface. By staying calm in the face of emotional intensity, by breathing steadily while experiencing the physical sensation of the feeling, by acknowledging your emotions, you can ride your wild horse, staying in control, constructively using the energy and vitality you will gain. As long as you continue to feel rather than think about your feelings, you will stay safely astride.

PART 3

Deepening

CHAPTER 8

Rage

The tigers of wrath are wiser than the horses of instruction.

—William Blake

As a child I experienced rage as a tangible entity. Rage had a personality—a shape, size, color, texture, sound. Like a stray cat looking for a handout, it simply attached itself to me or those I loved, too ugly and fierce to have been owned.

Rage is explosive, passionate, consuming. It is fury, momentary madness, anger gone berserk, the "urge to kill." Lying beneath its volcanic exterior are anger, outrage, fear, and despair; it is the result of the actual or threatened denial of basic needs. Infants turn fiery red and scream with rage when denied basic needs. As adults we fear its potential for destruction, we deny its demand for outlet. Yet rage is also the "fight" in the fight or flight response. It can inspire and empower us with both great physical strength and seemingly inexhaustible energy. Rage can save our lives as well as destroy them.

Need and Denial

Our feelings of rage were pushed into unconsciousness as we learned to hold our breath, clench our teeth, and squeeze our bodies to deaden the fierce emotion that surged toward the surface. We had to learn to suppress our rage to conform to society's definition of acceptable behavior, and suppressing rage made particular sense if our role models were volatile or abusive. We were persuaded, manipulated, cajoled, or punished into swallowing our natural feelings, especially rage, for rage frightens and enrages others as well. As a result, we became increasingly anesthetized to the very needs and feelings that triggered our rage in the first place.

Because rage is kindled by the survival force itself, it always will be an integral part of life's experience for each of us. But it is when we continue to deny rage that it festers and grows in our physical and mental consciousnesses. With the addition of each new denial, each new assault, a last straw eventually drops onto our emotional pile and we erupt, often harming ourselves and others. Our furious outbursts come as blasts; tempers snap and we lash out, red-faced, shaking. We smash and throw things. We yell, swear, and fight. At other times we boil and seethe just below the surface, our heads pounding, our stomachs in knots, our teeth gnashing, and our bodies stiffening until, painfully, we confine our furies to our inner world.

The inner expression of rage hurts us, at times drastically. Ongoing suppressed rage is the basis of such illnesses as hypertension, colitis, stroke, bursitis, migraines, and chronic back pain. The outward expression of rage hurts others, sometimes pathetically, tragically; wife beating, child beating, the abuse of the elderly or the infirm, are grizzly reminders of our potential for violence. Because of society's taboos, we often hold in our emotions during threatening situations and release them later once we feel safe. For example, should we fail to get the deserved recognition for our work or, worse yet, that praise were given to someone else, we would become resentful, angry. Rather than reveal our feelings to ourselves, much less publicly, we would push them inward, only to arrive home and vent our pain and frustration on our families.

Rage Terrifies

Whereas other intense emotions are *uncomfortable* to experience, rage is *terrifying*. It is the "final blow" that pushes us out of control. We feel irrational and panicky in its presence, yet rarely is the degree of our fury equal to the situation. Confronting the painful truth of our unfulfilled desires, our impotence to control every aspect of our lives, can create exaggerated and inappropriate responses. A puppy wets behind a chair, and we scream in outrage and slap the child who cares for the pet. We lose our car keys and, in our panic, yell, cry, throw things, or abusively accuse the household or office staff of conspiring against us.

Our belief that rage can be both internally and externally destructive results from a lifetime of accumulated frustrations. Incident after incident magnifies our irritation, yet we are unable or unwilling to reveal our true feelings, withholding them even from ourselves. In time our denial results in a prevailing sense of victimization. And because the display of emotion is so unacceptable in our culture, we often compound our fury by feeling guilty or by getting angry with ourselves for being angry. The line between sanity and insanity thins. When the dam breaks, the outcome is often frighteningly unexpected and destructive. We have lost control of our control. Is it any wonder we struggle so terribly to put the feelings of rage back in the now tightly sealed musculature of our bodies?

No one escapes feeling intensely frustrated from time to time. There always will be those moments when we feel impotent, unable to understand the seeming injustice of life. How we express our frustrations, however, how we experience the feelings of anger and rage, is a *choice* left solely to us, and it can run the gamut from open acceptance of a personal lesson to axe murder. The child can only flail and scream, but the adult can integrate intellect and feeling. (Refer to Chapter 6.) We may feel the same fury we did as tots, but now we can impose a dimension of rationality that will enable us to act appropriately and constructively in directing our most intense feelings.

Let Rage Be Your Teacher

The key to actualizing our feelings of rage is to *own* the raw emotion. We must take responsibility for our anger while remaining nonjudgmental of ourselves. Being closed and critical only turns our fury back upon ourselves. Resisting feelings of rage only escalates them. Rage is triggered by a sense of victimization and helplessness. But when we fully experience the intensity of our anger, we release the energy that will allow us to do something about the situation.

We all have experienced the growing frustrations of a day filled with added irritations. The water heater breaks, you miss an important phone call, you spill mustard on your new pants, your kids spend the morning arguing, you wait an hour to see the dentist, and your car refuses to start. You feel like screaming, your chest feels constricted, your jaw is set, and you think, 'If one more thing goes wrong, I'm going to explode!'' But wait! This is the opportunity to really *feel* your anger and acknowledge it. Feeling it in your body and admitting it to yourself—''God, I'm angry,'' ''I *feel* angry,'' ''So this is what my anger really feels like''—allow you to begin to release it.

Rage, like pain, is a guide, a teacher. Rage and its stepchildren anger, resentment, and sarcasm show us where our *protections* and *defenses* are the strongest, where we must work hardest. We are given the opportunity again and again to ask, ''What am I angry about?'' ''What threatens me?'' ''What am I afraid of?'' ''What basic needs are not being met?'' ''What am I denying myself—intimacy? nurturing? self-expression?'' An angry remark from parent to son may sound like ''Are you going to get a haircut soon or do you like looking like a Pomeranian?'' but may really mean ''I'm afraid I won't appear to be a good father, that I have lost control.'' When your wife asks, ''Honey, do you really want another drink?'' and you explode, hurling the glass against the wall and bellowing, ''Yeah, but where no one nags me,'' and slam out of the house, are you actually saying, ''I'm scared. Could I really be an alcoholic? Will she stick by me?'' Beneath the surface of rage lies a fear so frightening to consider that we transform the feeling directly into rage, sadness, grief—any emotion that is more easily dealt with and more societally acceptable.

Recognizing the Difference Between Emotion and Action

I would like to stress here that *experiencing* the feelings of rage and anger does not mean we must *act them out*. In fact, if we fully permit ourselves to experience the feelings as they arise, we ensure that the behavior that follows our emotional responses will be in proportion to the cause, appropriate to the situation, and will support us in our intention to stay open and fully functioning.

Acknowledging deep-seated rage and anger puts us in touch with life-threatening problems, shows us the depth of our denial of physical and emotional feeling, and reflects the enormous amount of potential energy we have for positive, constructive action, for creativity, for vitality. Unlike a drowning man who fights the water until he succumbs, we must relax and flow with the tide to save ourselves.

The exercises that follow may overwhelm you, but so does rage. Eventually you will come to trust staying open even in the face of emotional storms, at first during the exercises and later through the ups and downs of daily living. Anger and frustration will no longer be so devastatingly frightening. You will not have to wait until the last straw forces you into a confrontation; you will stay current with each new situation; you will make your rage work for you, not against you.

When you stop using your will and emotional strength to push your rage into unconsciousness, power and energy are released. A potential for creative action fills the spaces that were occupied by tightness and tension; and, like any other intense emotion, rage comes to be experienced as an internal guide to well-being.

Rage Quiz

Quickly, without mulling over your answers, circle the felt response, remembering that once again this is simply an exercise in information collecting. Answers are neither right nor wrong, good nor bad.

1. People who are very angry are out of control.   T   F
2. Intense anger is childish.   T   F
3. Rage is bad.   T   F
4. Intense anger is immoral.   T   F
5. It makes me angry to see someone else getting angry.   T   F
6. It frightens me when I feel rage.   T   F
7. It frightens me when people get angry with me.   T   F
8. When I feel rage, I hold it inside.   T   F
9. When I feel very frustrated, I cry.   T   F
10. When I feel angry, I yell.   T   F
11. When I feel angry, I take it out on my family.   T   F
12. When I feel rage, I get a headache.   T   F
13. When I feel very frustrated, I escape from the feelings by drinking or eating.   T   F
14. I was never permitted to show rage as a child.   T   F
15. I feel angry most of the time.   T   F
16. I often feel like having a temper tantrum.   T   F
17. When someone blows up at me, I run away.   T   F
18. I never get angry.   T   F
19. When I'm angry, I often say things I don't mean.   T   F
20. I don't let anger build up inside of me; I deal with it as it happens.   T   F

21. Anger is ugly.	T	F
22. Spiritual (religious) people never get angry.	T	F
23. I feel guilty after I have been mad at someone.	T	F
24. Showing my rage makes me feel powerful.	T	F
25. It's okay for me to get angry and express it.	T	F
26. Women never get intensely angry.	T	F
27. Rage excites me.	T	F
28. It takes me a long time to get over my anger.	T	F
29. It's okay to use drugs to get rid of anger.	T	F
30. It is difficult for me to express anger directly to a stranger.	T	F
31. I yell and scream a lot.	T	F
32. I find it easier to get angry with those people who are closest to me.	T	F
33. I like to hurt people verbally when I'm angry.	T	F
34. My parents often were angry with me.	T	F
35. When I feel rage, I can stop it with a few drinks.	T	F

Fill in the blanks with the first words (don't use more than two) that come to mind.

1. It makes me feel _____ to see someone angry.
2. I'm afraid to make people angry with me because they will _____ me.
3. People who feel rage are _____.
4. The parent I felt the most rage from was my _____.
5. In my family, rage was usually expressed by _____.
6. When I feel rage, I use my anger to _____.
7. I can stop feeling rage by _____ or _____.
8. When I feel frustrated, I blot out my feelings by _____.
9. The best way to handle rage is to _____.
10. If I got angry enough, I could _____.
11. When I feel angry toward someone I love, I _____.
12. When I feel angry toward someone I barely know, I _____.
13. When my mother was angry with me, she _____.
14. When my father was angry with me, he _____.
15. The most frightening thing about rage is _____.

Exercises for Rage

1. Refer to the exercise in Chapter 7. Complete this exercise using the experience of rage as your focus. If as you begin to experience the intensity of your felt rage you go numb, uncritically shift your focus to an intense exploration of what non-feeling feels like. (You may wish to refer to Chaper 10.)

2. If you are too agitated to lie down or sit quietly as you follow your breath to the source of intensity within your body, *take a walk, run, or hike up a mountain; repeat the first exercise while "moving." Let the rhythm of your movement guide your breath and bring it to the spot in your body that holds the most rage.* Keep the focus on your body; do not make this an intellectual exercise. Delete judgment and criticism. If you tire or stop, do not stop breathing or focusing on the feeling. Continue your focus as you return home.

3. If you tend to unconsciously diminish your breathing as your emotional intensity rises, try this: *Tap or press on your chest as a reminder to continue breathing steadily as you proceed with the exercises.* Do this any time you feel the need to be reminded.

4. After you have spent time focusing on the raw feeling of rage, ask yourself any or all of the following questions, answering them as fully and spontaneously as possible. Try not to think about your responses; just allow whatever surfaces to have expression.

- *Could this rage be covering up my feelings of sadness, grief, or fear? How far back can I remember feeling this emotion?* Allow any images, sounds, voices, etc., that come up to be accepted as helpful and healing information. Let the images play themselves out.
- *Do I remember anyone who also felt this way or made me feel this way? Who or what is the source of my rage? What would I like to say to this person or thing?*

CHAPTER 9

Pain and Grief

And a woman spoke, saying, Tell us of Pain.
And he said:
Your pain is the breaking of the shell that encloses
your understanding.

—Kahlil Gibran

Pain Serves a Purpose

The function of pain is to sustain and protect life. Its shrill alarm alerts us to danger. Pain, be it physical or emotional, is functional, purposeful, and must be acknowledged. We urgently need to take our hand off the stove, come in out of the cold, deal with injury, meet our needs, stop pushing love away, and allow our divided selves to be integrated. Pain is the signal to take notice, to wake up, to act, to open; and the way we tend to react to bodily pain can reveal hidden assumptions and beliefs about ourselves.

Emotional pain and suffering, particularly grief, generate from the belief that something irreplaceable has been denied, something of great value has been lost. I have heard many say they will "never attain the life they want," "never get another chance like that," "have lost the best job they could ever have," or "will never love again." Their best friend, their support, their love, or their purpose in life is gone. Devastated, deeply depressed, they believe they are absolutely alone and have lost their dreams, their goals, their hopes.

Grief and intense pain are so closely linked as to be inseparable. They are, perhaps, the most painful of emotions to bear. One feels an emptiness, a hollowness, a longing that borders on sickness. We all have experienced this to some degree. It is not only an emotion felt at the loss of a loved one, but also the deep desire for life to be different from the way it is. Or as Stephen Levine so aptly put it in *A Gradual Awakening*, ''wanting things to be otherwise is the very essence of suffering.'' All our longings seem to have a shroud of grief draped around them.

Pain Can Be Disguised

Emotional pain and grief, like all feelings, can be pushed from conscious awareness or converted into far more easily tolerated emotions. If the feelings of vulnerability that our pain causes are too threatening, we can transform the pain into rage, mask it with humor, or deaden it with food, alcohol, drugs, or compulsive behaviors. To some degree, however, emotional and physical pain are ever-present when we feel any hurt. Interestingly, people who experience a great deal of physical pain do not tend to suffer as acutely from emotional pain. The reverse is also true: Those who experience intense emotional pain are not as likely to suffer great physical distress. The patterns emphasizing one experience of pain over the other tend to develop in families, the legacy being handed down from generation to generation.

Pain Carries an Important Message

Pain is to be avoided in our society, which consumes thousands of pounds of aspirin daily. The tranquilizer Valium, used to calm emotional pain, is the number one prescription drug in this country. Pain of any type frightens us, and our resistance to it is a mental and physical tightening. We close around the pain, magnifying it. But pain is our teacher—a ferocious one at that, but our teacher nonetheless.

Physical pain, signaling the breakdown of homeostasis, which maintains the subtle balance of life in the body, can come as a reaction to injury or disease, and often follows closely on the heels of emotional suffering. Intense or chronic pain, particularly that which cannot be justified or explained through physical causes, has long been a puzzlement to medicine, since it appears to lack a message or guide function in the body. There is just ''no physical explanation for it.'' Today, much successful work with this kind of pain has had a psychological focus. Chronic pain patients are asked to consider that their pain may be a way of not dealing with their lives.

We, of course, have all used pain as an excuse for nonaction—"I can't go to the party tonight, I don't feel well enough," "Can I stay home from school today, Mom? I feel sick. I can take the test tomorrow," "Not tonight, dear, I have a headache." Long-time sufferers are asked to reflect on their responses to such questions as "What message about my life does this pain convey?" "What lesson do I need to learn?" "What am I afraid to do that is important to me?" "What am I hiding from?" The root cause of their suffering often runs into their worst fear and dread. But the wisdom of this approach to pain in regard to relentless physical as well as emotional suffering was dramatically revealed to me early in my work with cancer.

Eddie, a very loving and protective man in his early forties, was dying of cancer of the lymphatic system. He had put up a truly courageous fight for several years but had finally grown weary. Leaving the hospital, he returned home to die.

Eddie had carefully examined and radically improved many areas of his life. Although his relationships with friends and family had blossomed, he had been unable to alter his relationship with his wife, Ann. He loved her deeply and she him, but the specter of death and her unwillingness to confront her grief and fear lay like a deep and bridgeless gap between them. I too tried many times to engage Ann in conversation about her husband, but she simply refused to speak about him with me or anyone. I understood how deeply she was suffering and hoped that sooner or later she would reach out for the help and support she so desperately needed.

One afternoon shortly after Eddie left the hospital, I received a frantic call from Ann. Eddie was in such agony that he could neither sit nor lie down. All he could do was pace the floor, moaning and crying. Everything medically possible to alleviate the pain had been done. The nerve endings connected to the areas in his throat and shoulder, which were the source of the pain, had been severed. Yet the pain intensified. Even the strongest opiates produced little relief.

I had absolutely no idea how to improve the situation, but I too loved Eddie and so set out on the long drive to his home, praying all the way for guidance. I arrived just as he had fallen into his first sleep in days. Later, it occurred to me that perhaps he had fallen asleep when he heard my car pull into the driveway, knowing that what he needed would somehow, some way, be taken care of.

I found myself alone with Ann in the kitchen. We shared our grief and concern over the agony that seemed relentless and that left both of us feeling hopeless and impotent. On a hunch, I asked her once again if she would be willing to speak openly about her fears and concerns, and listen to her husband's as well. "All of them?" she asked hesitantly. "All," I replied, "including the fact that Eddie is likely to die soon." She paused for several moments and then in a clear, strong voice replied, "I'll do anything that would ease my husband's suffering."

Eddie awoke shortly after and called us to come to him. Tears filled my eyes as I witnessed what was surely a triumph of love over fear. For the next several hours the three of us explored with great thoroughness every concern, every emotion, every uncertainty, every fear either of them had about dying, death, what would come after, how she would manage, the children, his parents. They also shared the joy and gratitude they felt in having known and loved each other. To this day I consider those few hours among the most beautiful and relevant in my life.

After that conversation, Eddie's pain abruptly came to an end. He died ten days later in perfect peace, surrounded by people he loved. His head was cradled in his father's hands, Ann's hands were in his over his heart. Eddie's agony had been a message that he profoundly needed to convey his thoughts and feelings to his wife, to feel her acceptance, her strength, and her love. Unfortunately, his pain had to assume agonizing proportions; yet, without it, he never would have had the opportunity to resolve the conflict with his wife, which then led to so tranquil a death.

Fear Makes Pain Hurt More

Eddie's story also points to the fact that much of what we experience as pain is anxiety, dread of the future. People sometimes find themselves in the convoluted situation of being in pain because they fear the future holds even more.

When my son was little, he agonized for hours before his appointment with the pediatrician for his shots. Once in the office, he made life such hell for all concerned that it usually took two hefty nurses to hold him still long enough for the doctor to prick him with the needle. Afterward, he was fine, but I went home and took to my bed with two aspirin and a cold cloth.

His younger sister was not any fonder of shots, but she responded quite differently. Even as a toddler, she would march into the doctor's office, stick out her arm, shriek once when the needle was inserted, and then happily continue with the rest of the examination.

Clearly, the amount of suffering my son endured was far greater than that of his sister. Her pain had to do with being pricked physically, and it was over in a blink of an eye. His pain was based on memories of similar past experiences—pain that sprang from terrified expectations of the future and that lasted for hours. It always turned out as badly as he imagined it would.

Most people's pain results from the consequence of their struggle against the experience, not the experience itself. So often the worst part about any unpleasant, unavoidable event is the anticipation or expectation of what will happen. Because we feel tense and anxious, we tighten and constrain our bodies in ways that in themselves produce pain and suffering. In situations where we cannot run, cannot fight, and will not surrender to the experience, we often resist in ways that ensure an experience of what we dread most.

Again, you are probably at the point of asking, "So what?" The problem may have been ably diagnosed, but how do you handle the agony once you are in the midst of it? To simply tell someone that his/her pain is psychosomatic does not in any way diminish it.

By now you might have guessed that my recommendation for appropriately treating pain is the same as my recommendation for treating all intense feelings: Face it; go into it; experience it; and the process will set you free.

David, a sensitive young man in his twenties, introduced himself to me with this statement: "If I can't get some relief from this pain, I'm going to kill myself." For over a year and a half he had lived day in and day out with unrelentingly severe pelvic pain, a result of a severe infection in his groin. The infection had healed, yet his suffering had continued. His pain had been unsuccessfully treated medically and could be neither explained nor understood. David had consulted with a number of competent doctors, all of whom assured him that the pain was due to his nerves. He was given tranquilizers and muscle relaxants, which made him sleepy but did not reduce his distress.

When he came to me, I asked him to consider what he thought about most of the time. His response was "tomorrow's pain, and pain the day after, and the day after that." He actually spent most of his time fearing pain that was "coming." I suggested that he engage in the simple exercise I recommended earlier in the book—and continue to recommend—to create a safe, private, comfortable environment; to relax himself with the breathing technique; and then to focus on the part of his body that housed the pain. He did this exercise for sixty minutes daily without thinking about or analyzing anything, just experiencing his pain.

David found that when he stopped thinking about his suffering in a past or future context and, instead, directed his attention to the sensation itself, the pain diminished to a point where it was bearable.

This victory was not the end for David; it was only the beginning. As a consequence of living in the moment, he began facing the many important issues in his life that he had been avoiding. He continues to face them, and he continues to be free of this particular pain. What David did in focusing on his pain was to open himself up to the understanding that it was not only the pain in his body that he had resisted; it was also the self-doubt, the self-criticism, and the fear that had imprisoned him.

This same principle holds true for emotional pain. Fear, like pain, closes our minds as well as our hearts. When we experience our sadness, our grief, our anger, our deepest fears, we are, quite literally, healing ourselves.

To live is to risk pain from time to time. Learning to appropriately experience pain does not remove it from our lives, but it does free us from protections that constrict and diminish the quality of our lives. Once we embrace our resistance to pain and grief, we discover a messenger that can direct us to paths of renewed energy, enthusiasm, compassion, and joy.

Pain and Grief Quiz

Answer the following questions by consulting your physical and emotional feelings. Again, there are no correct answers to any of the following questions, only points of departure.

Circle the answer that best describes how you feel.

1. I spend a lot of time in pain.   T F
2. I'm rarely depressed.   T F
3. My life is full of meaning and purpose.   T F
4. I'm afraid that tomorrow won't be any better than today.   T F
5. I rarely think about my losses.   T F
6. I often talk about my aches and pains.   T F
7. I expect life to be painful.   T F
8. I never have felt grief.   T F
9. I try to ignore my physical pains.   T F
10. I never focus on anything that is negative.   T F
11. I would rather not feel than feel bad.   T F
12. When I hurt myself, I usually ignore it.   T F

13. I frequently use sickness as an excuse.   T F
14. I need drugs to ease my pain.   T F
15. I suffer much more emotionally than physically.   T F
16. My mother often complained of aches and pains.   T F
17. I can't remember the last time I wasn't in pain.   T F
18. I always can find some way to numb bodily pain.   T F
19. I think suffering silently is noble.   T F
20. I'm afraid to talk about my pain.   T F
21. I fear being in pain more than anything.   T F
22. Going to the dentist terrifies me.   T F
23. I will do anything to avoid unpleasantness.   T F
24. Men can withstand hardship better than women can.   T F
25. I can't bear to be around anyone who is in pain.   T F
26. I usually let my pain run its course naturally.   T F
27. Strong people don't complain about their pain.   T F
28. I believe pain has something to teach me.   T F
29. Life is hard and full of pain.   T F
30. When I'm in pain, I feel out of control.   T F
31. I never have felt intense pain of any kind.   T F
32. I use alcohol as a painkiller.   T F

List five ways you control your physical pain.

List five ways you control your emotional discomfort.

List several experiences that have caused you grief.

Write your immediate response in the space provided using only one or two words.

1. When I think about pain, I'm reminded of _____.
2. The physical pain of others makes me feel _____.

3. I feel grief most often in my _____.
4. The worst pain I can remember as a child was when I was _____ years old.
5. My family dealt with physical pain by _____.
6. The worst kind of pain is _____.
7. The worst thing about pain is that it makes me feel _____.
8. I feel pain most often in my _____ and my _____.
9. People who give in to their pain are _____.
10. I feel _____ when I am around people who are grieving.
11. The thing I fear most about pain is _____.
12. When I feel grief, I _____.
13. People who talk about their pain are _____.
14. The most intense physical pain I have ever felt was in my _____.
15. The most intense emotional pain I have ever felt was when _____.
16. I push my feelings of loss away by _____.
17. Women deal with pain by _____.
18. Men deal with pain by _____.
19. When I was a child, my family expressed grief by _____.
20. I feel comfortable sharing my grief with _____.
21. When I lose something of great value, I _____.
22. If I could change my life this moment, I would _____ _____.
23. The physical excuse I usually use for nonaction is that I'm _____.
24. I would rather feel the emotion of _____ than grief.
25. People hurt me the most by _____ me.

Exercises for Pain and Grief

Keep in mind that the point of the exercises that follow is to relieve you of the burdensome and limiting habit of investing a great deal of energy in *not* knowing and *not* feeling.

BASIC EXERCISE

Refer to the exercise in Chapter 7. Complete this exercise using the experience of pain or grief as your focus. You may wish to experience them in combination. Pain and grief are so closely linked that they may be experienced simultaneously.

ADDITIONAL EXERCISES

1. If you are experiencing physical pain, itching, or some other intense bodily discomfort, direct your breath and attention to an ever-diminishing area of distress (the forearm, for instance). Visualize the area as a circle. *Spend a minute or two breathing into the pain, focusing on it.* Continuing on, try to locate the part of the circle of pain that is the most intense (perhaps just above the wrist). Again, continue breathing rhythmically and focus your attention on this area for a couple of minutes. *Next, determine the center of this circle where the pain is most intense* (try to visualize the spot where the pain seems to intensify) and *go on breathing into it, experiencing this new point of discomfort.* Keep your focus on this area for a few minutes. *Continue in this way, focusing and breathing into each new center as each new single point decreases in circumference until the nucleus of the pain becomes so minute as to be impossible to visualize and the point of discomfort diminishes or disappears entirely.*

2. Experience the type of pain you are having (whether the cause is physical or emotional) by asking yourself the following questions while breathing fully and deeply. Open yourself to the feelings and sensations that will arise as you focus and breathe into them.

- *What does the sensation of this pain feel like? Hot? Cold? Tearing? Aching? Dull? Cramping? Shrill?*
- *What is the quality of the sensation? Is it solid? Does it have weight? Color? Does it move around or stay in one place? Is it constant or intermittent? Is it round? Soft? Flat? Textured?*
- *Does the sensation seem to come from one point or are there several points? Are there many levels and sensations or only one? Do they vary in intensity?*
- *Does the sensation of the pain remind me of anything?*

Continue breathing and focusing on your answers. Stay open to any pictures, sounds, colors, feelings, etc., that come up for you. Let your body describe the sensations of pain to you.

3. There are times, as when someone you love has died or is slowly dying, that pain and grief seem interminable. Months or even years may pass as you stand by helplessly watching a loved one die of a terminal illness. Again, permitting yourself to experience your feelings of grief, anger, and helplessness will make it possible for you to cope with difficult situations. During the tough times when you feel like screaming, shouting, crying hysterically, or when you feel you are going crazy, *breathe steadily into the emotion by locating the place in your body that houses its greatest intensity. Focus and breathe, breathe and focus.* If you feel, not think, about your emotions, you will find that even in the most chaotic of situations, your head will be clear, your heart will be open, and you will intuitively know how to behave.

4. If feelings of pain and grief linger without apparent cause, direct the following questions to the source of your feelings.

- *Could these feelings be anger instead of grief?*
- *If they are, with whom am I angry?* Acknowledge the answer that surfaces from your feeling self even if it happens to be someone who has died or is ill or disabled. Allow the feelings of anger at this person or event, however irrational they may seem, to intensify and be experienced.
- *Could these feelings be fear instead of grief? If so, of what am I afraid?* Accept whatever surfaces and direct your breathing to the source of the feelings you have uncovered.

CHAPTER 10

Numbing

You must feel everything,
otherwise the world loses its meaning.
                    —Carlos Castaneda

The story of Rip Van Winkle, the fellow who fell asleep for one hundred years, is a popular folktale. Everyone can identify to some extent with the theme of sleeping life away. In this day and age, turning off has, in fact, become a national pastime.

We have become enormously clever—ingenious, in fact— in devising brilliant schemes to turn off our emotions and tune out physical sensations. We have created myriad ways to silence, numb, deaden, and withdraw from our feelings. The irony, however, is that these strategies, originally intended to protect us, now have become habituated, compulsive, and, in some extreme cases, even lethal.

We work and play under headphones, drive enveloped in elaborate stereo systems, and snap on the television as soon as we walk through our front doors. Out comes the food, the alcohol, the grass, as we binge, drink, and drug ourselves out of loneliness and isolation and into semi-consciousness. We sleep too much, get sick too often, chatter endlessly, move, drive, and work ourselves relentlessly in a frantic attempt to shut out sadness, grief, and rage. We push ourselves to the edge of sanity rather than allow ourselves to be aware of what we feel within. In short, we pretend to live. Instead of enthusiastically experiencing life, we shun it like a lepers' colony, all the while searching almost desperately to find new ways to block out what we cannot forget or forgive—namely, our suffering.

Exchanging a Full Palette for a Few Gray Tones

When we first choose *not* to feel, we invariably are too young to realize that what we are doing is exchanging the full palette of sensations for a few gray ones. Non-feeling is a result of shaving off the peaks and valleys of emotional intensity. It is, at best, an experience of flatness, of sameness, of uniformity, a life of white bread and boiled potatoes. But at the very edge of non-feeling is a subtle, barely perceptible tinge of emptiness and sadness that is ever-present. It is a distant memory, a dim recognition that keeps reminding us that something is missing, something is wrong.

To protect ourselves from what we fear, we have maimed our emotional selves by shutting down and, as a result, have dramatically diminished our capacity to experience life—to see, hear, taste, touch, and smell. In so doing we have stunted our sensitivity, creativity, productivity, and vitality.

Numbing Can Be Lethal

People who withdraw have numbed themselves; they have made arrangements and accommodations; they have companions, acquaintances, sex partners. They do not have soul mates, intimates, or lovers. Unfortunately, the sacrifices we make to protect ourselves prove worthless in the long run. Our feelings refuse to be muffled. Life and health demand that we pay attention to the messages they convey. In spite of our efforts to silence them, these messages grow louder and stronger until, eventually, they force themselves to the surface. By then the cost of denying them often is devastating. As we attempt to devise increasingly elaborate defenses, they consume more and more of our energy and health. In time, the distinction between a living process and a dying process becomes so fine as to be nonexistent. At this point, I believe, it is easy to succumb to serious illness.

I had a friend, Jerry, who recently died of cancer. He was nineteen. Jerry's life story was very much like that of several other people I have known and with whom I have worked. Most were teenagers; all were quiet, withdrawn, and emotionally dead. Shortly before his death, Jerry wrote a touching story about how having cancer had evoked the emotions he had all but forgotten. His story began with a description of himself before he became ill. He created a picture of a tall, gangling boy whose nose was always buried in a book. During recess and lunch periods, he sat off to the side, reading. He was always alone, whether at home with his family or at the beach with his friends. He did not know how to express his feelings; he barely knew they existed. Jerry wrote of listening to the diagnosis of his cancer without feeling any emotion whatsoever. It was not until later, when he was told that the medical intervention had not succeeded in halting the progression of his disease, that the tears and emotions within him finally surfaced.

Jerry's surgery and his subsequent first round of radiation and chemotherapy had passed by as if they were happening to someone else. But during and after the intensely difficult days of his second round of therapy, when he euphemistically described himself as "coughing in Technicolor," he found within the pages of a journal he started keeping the friend he had always longed for, the friend who could feel his pain and understand. This friend was simply the vulnerable, lonely, and intensely sad boy whom Jerry had so long ago locked away from consciousness. To his delight, Jerry found that this friend could also laugh and play and nurture him.

Jerry wrote voluminously, delighting in the fact that, for the first time in his life, he was able to express all that he felt. He submitted an article that was published in the school paper. In it he told of finding this wonderful lost part of himself because of his having cancer.

When I am with people like Jerry, and I have been with many of all ages, I ask myself, "Is this what it takes to open people to the fact that they have hidden, locked away, or forgotten a treasure of incalculable value—their feelings? Do they always have to be taken to the precipice before they are willing to confront who they are?" In the end, the most life-threatening feelings are the consequence of the decision not to feel. Life is a process that never stands still, never levels off. The decision to feel, no matter how painful or frightening, is a decision to extend our lives. The decision to numb, to withdraw, to escape, is one that undermines this intention.

Again the questions surface: What do you do with your numbness after you have spent a lifetime manufacturing it? Can you really deal with the discomfort of uncontrollable emotion? How do you integrate emotion into your life once you find the high and low notes? Believing, at last, that as an adult you simply *can* handle them is an enormous first step. *Know* that your feelings, no matter how deadened or denied, are still there. Just because you have not heard the notes does not mean the instrument will not play.

Not Feeling Is a Feeling

The key is to treat the experience of non-feeling exactly as I have suggested you treat intense feeling, that is, to simply observe throughout the day your non-feeling response from a perspective of understanding and compassion. If you have turned off, you had good reasons for doing so. Be gentle with yourself.

When using the time you have set aside, focus on the place in your body where the numbness is most obvious and breathe into this area. Continue to meditate this way on the center of your deadness. Resist the temptation to think about or analyze the situation. Of course, your attention will wander; but each time it does, gently bring it back to the same area of your body on which you have chosen to focus. Do not expect miracles. It has taken you a long time to develop the habit of shutting out feeling, and it will take time to learn new patterns. At the very least, you are deeply relaxing and de-stressing yourself with this practice of concentration.

Eventually, as you continue to focus on your body, your trust in it and in yourself will grow. Your fear of being overwhelmed by fear and loneliness or of losing control will give way to your acceptance of life and its full range of emotional experiences.

Quiz on Numbing

The following questions suggest ways in which you may be numbing and hiding from yourself. Let your physical and emotional feelings direct the responses you give as you keep in mind that here once again is another information-collecting process. Circle the answer that best describes how you feel.

1. I get sick often.   T   F
2. I have great difficulty expressing anger.   T   F
3. I always have a drink when I get home from work. T   F

4. My meals rarely satisfy me.   T   F
5. I almost never feel sad.   T   F
6. I watch television several hours each day.   T   F
7. I rarely feel loving.   T   F
8. I love the feeling of exercising and moving.   T   F
9. I have close friends.   T   F
10. Reading is my only pastime activity.   T   F
11. I am an observer in life rather than a participant.   T   F
12. I enjoy a good cry occasionally.   T   F
13. I have a gratifying sex life.   T   F
14. I rarely feel vulnerable.   T   F
15. If I concentrate for a moment, I can be aware of
    almost any part of my body.   T   F
16. Nothing in life seems to excite me.   T   F
17. I need medication to help me sleep.   T   F
18. I am depressed frequently.   T   F
19. I can't get through a day without drinking or using
    drugs.   T   F
20. I have a reputation for being "cool."   T   F
21. My energy level is usually low.   T   F
22. I have never felt grief.   T   F
23. I often feel empty.   T   F
24. I breathe shallowly most of the time.   T   F
25. I rarely seem to enjoy life.   T   F

Fill in the letter code of the word that best applies (Never—N,
Occasionally—O, Usually—U, Frequently—F, Always—A).

1. I'm _____ aware of how my body feels.
2. I _____ feel healthy and strong.
3. I _____ smoke when I'm nervous.
4. I'm _____ in pain physically.
5. I'm _____ able to express my feelings of anger.
6. I _____ use alcoholic beverages.
7. I _____ enjoy having sex.
8. I feel tired _____.
9. I _____ get enough exercise.
10. I _____ feel upset with myself.
11. I _____ felt warm and loved as a child.
12. I have _____ felt grief.
13. I _____ feel good about myself.
14. I _____ sleep well.

15. I _____ feel empty.
16. I cry _____.
17. I _____ feel love.
18. I _____ feel afraid.
19. I _____ feel vital and alive.
20. I'm _____ aware of my feelings.

Exercises for Numbing

As you engage in these exercises, remember that your goal is awareness. Change will follow automatically as perception, unencumbered by criticism or judgment, steadily grows.

BASIC EXERCISE

Non-feeling is often more terrifying than any intensely felt emotion, but the process for releasing non-feeling is exactly the same. (Refer to Chapter 7.) *First locate the place in your body where you feel the greatest emptiness.* Often it is the chest, stomach, or pelvis, but it can be anywhere. Take your time as you breathe steadily and deeply into the part of your body that feels the emptiest. Continue to breathe steadily into the area, focusing all your attention there. Follow your breath to this spot during the entire time you have allotted for this exercise. *If your mind wanders, gently bring it back, again and again, if necessary.* Following the format prescribed in Chapter 7, let the experience of emptiness deepen and intensify.

ADDITIONAL EXERCISES

1. If you grow angry, frustrated, or frightened in the process of experiencing your numbness, begin to *direct your focus and breathe into these feelings.* Intensify them in the way described in Chapter 7.

2. If you have become aware that you use food, alcohol, television, whatever, to numb your feelings, try the following

procedure: *The next time you would like to do something compulsive or inappropriate in order to numb your feelings, focus on the feelings that provoked this urge.* Follow the procedure outlined in Chapter 7.

3. *Become an uncritical observer of the ways you numb yourself throughout the day.* Notice what you do with intense feelings as they arise, and try to find out precisely how you discount or disguise them.

CHAPTER 11

Fear, Love, and Freedom

The needle that pierces may carry a thread that binds us to heaven.

—James Hastings

''Beauty and the Beast,'' along with ''The Frog Prince'' and other stories of this genre, were my childhood favorites; I reveled in their magic. Only recently, though, did I come to appreciate fully the profound and deeply personal message they convey. Beauty, the heroine, represents all that is good, noble, and loving. She is forced to leave the safety of her home and live, instead, with the Beast; otherwise her father will die. The Beast, through Beauty's eyes, is a creature whose physical hideousness and fearful power she can hardly bear. Drawing upon all her will and strength, she forces herself to stay with the creature. To her complete surprise, she grows to care for him, sensing the softness and vulnerability beneath his terrifying exterior. Later, as he lies dying, Beauty realizes that she loves the Beast. At that moment the monster transforms, revealing himself to be a handsome prince, as the power of Beauty's love breaks the terrible spell that has been placed on him. And, as is apropos of fairy tales, Beauty and the Beast embrace and live happily ever after.

This lovely fable is a powerful metaphor of the inner journey each of us must take throughout our lives and especially of the journey of transformation you are taking as outlined by this book. When we recognize the necessity and summon up the will and the courage to confront and experience the most terrifying ''monster'' in our lives—our own fear of the unknown—we discover a depth of love, compassion, and beauty hidden within.

Fear Underlies Protections

Again and again, as we permit ourselves to open to the source of our most dreaded emotions, fear awaits us—fear of worthlessness, of abandonment, of death, of nothingness. As we have seen, fear arising from the past and projected into the future is the source of our ongoing pain and grief, the generator of chronic depression and rage. It is the "good reason" behind the protective responses and behaviors that no longer are rewarding yet continue to influence, even to dominate, our lives.

As we come to recognize the disturbing feelings that underlie and trigger our self-limiting patterns, we grow immeasurably in understanding and compassion. We are not "bad"; we are frightened. With this understanding, we see ourselves as we are rather than as we pretend to be. With compassion for ourselves and a willingness to experience fear itself, we take a giant step forward in our transformational journey.

Adults Can Deal with Fear in Ways That Children Cannot

So far, we have followed a path that has led from observation to understanding, from understanding to compassion, and from compassion to awareness. Although little may seem to have outwardly changed, we have been set free. Awareness and acceptance of our fearfulness have not erased that feeling, but they have given us access to unlimited options. *We* are now in charge, not our fear. In the years since our deepest fears took hold, we all have added enormously to our stockpile of personal resources. In addition to feeling, we are also intellect, will, and intuition. Since our youth, when we began to limit ourselves by anesthetizing our physical and emotional selves, we have been given repeated opportunities to reverse this pattern whenever those same feelings surfaced. If we could not have handled our feelings in the past, we can *now*, though the intensity of feeling may still be frightening. We will not die; we will not go mad. By reconnecting our full range of physical and emotional feeling to rational awareness, we produce the personal strength it takes to face and go beyond our deepest fears.

As I willingly permitted intimacy to become a part of my life, as I stopped denying its presence by my thoughts and behaviors, the deepest of my fears surfaced, and what I found was a vast and ancient reservoir of tremendous vulnerability. I began to experience all the fear that I had so carefully hidden from my consciousness. Again and again I was put in touch with the feelings of a grief-stricken child who believed she was an unlovable nonentity. Intimacy always brought this very frightening, very irrational part of me to the surface; I always feared it and, therefore, avoided it. Now instead, I *made* myself stand my emotional ground. I *made* myself relive those overwhelming feelings of worthlessness and heartache that risking closeness instantly triggered. It took time—time and considerable effort—to release the tremendous amount of pain and fear that had been buried for so long. But each time I did so, those feelings became less overwhelming and I was less fearful than the time before. Each time I gained more confidence, I became more compassionate and more loving with myself. Most importantly, I stopped being afraid of the experience of fear. I *proved* to myself I could survive my worst fears—and if I could, anyone could.

Energy, Vitality, and Freedom Are the Rewards for Facing Fear

Choosing to do things differently, even things that will make us feel good, often is difficult. In time, new patterns replace the old, but the changing of the guard will neither feel natural nor be easy. We are creatures of habit. We love comfort, safety, and predictability. What is it, then, that pushes us? Where do we find the resources to climb up and go out of our emotional trenches?

In the doing, no matter how awkward it may seem at first, lies the source of our own energy. The more fear we uncover, the more vitality and enthusiasm we expose. Rarely do we have any idea of the enormous amount of energy it takes *not* to feel, not to know, to press into unconsciousness what is painful and frightening. Once this energy is no longer diverted and blocked, it is available for positive, rewarding behaviors. As we experience the release of sadness, pain, and fear, we also feel the boundless resource of our energy. We feel our confidence rising. We experience the full extent of our strength and capacity to feel alive. We are also rewarded by the love and devotion we begin to inspire in others. The more we are free to feel, the more charismatic we become.

Once we have faced the frightening realities of the past, it becomes easier to face the "frightening" possibilities of the future, for it is in experiencing the *feeling* of fear that we break its power over us. We realize that we are not dealing with an uncontrollable monster bent on crushing us. Each time we meet the challenge to acknowledge our fear, we grow stronger, more vital, more self-assured. We even begin to look for the challenges, the lessons, that ultimately will enhance the quality of our lives.

Love Surfaces as Fear Dissolves

But this is not the end. It is, in fact, the wondrous beginning. There is more to come than you could ever imagine. If fear were a stone you could crack open, inside you would find buried a gem of indescribable worth and beauty—and that would be love.

Matter cannot be destroyed—only transformed. When something dies, something else fills that void. Life moves on. I realize that when you are in a state of fear, it seems implausible, ludicrous perhaps, that love and compassion are housed within you. Yet time after time, whether by choice or circumstances you confront your deepest fears, the emotions that remain are joy, gratitude, and love.

Those of us who have worked with the seriously ill and dying often are fortunate to have watched their remarkable transition from a state of fear to one of love. I routinely have seen bitter, angry, terrified individuals look death in the face as they learned to open to and embrace their fear. I have felt them soften and grow increasingly radiant, tranquil, and appreciative as they began to participate in life. Moreover, it seems to matter little whether afterward they have lived or soon died.

I have learned that in order to love, we need not work at loving. There is nothing to do. But we do have to work at acknowledging the painful and frightening emotions from which we hide. This process does not involve destroying the "undesirable" parts of ourselves, as that is impossible. Rather, it demands that we acknowledge, understand, and integrate the very emotions we loathe, that we expose the dark side of ourselves to the light. When I confronted my deepest fears, I was facing the shadowy recesses that were connected to an enormous amount of pain. Yet each time I faced those fears, I became more appreciative of the gift of my own life.

When we have met and risked the "Beast," we find beneath its terrifying exterior our own beauty, compassion, understanding, and appreciation for all of life. We see our playfulness, our enthusiasm, our curiosity, our boundless energy. We discover our depth of caring for others and for life itself. We need only to continue in our willingness to open more widely, to feel more intensely, to see more clearly. At those times when our lives are the most difficult, we are provided with the opportunity to further expand the limits of our self-awareness, to risk going beyond fear to a depth of love we might never have imagined possible.

PART 4

Awakening

CHAPTER 12

Life After Fear

To conquer fear is the beginning of wisdom.
—Bertrand Russell

A young Zen monk asked his master, who was chopping wood, "Master, what did you do before your enlightenment?" The old man replied, "I chopped wood." The young monk thought for a moment and then continued, "Well, then, what did you do after your enlightenment?" His master's eyes twinkled. "I chopped more wood."

Life After Fear Takes on New Meaning

Life after fear has been confronted can be lived more fully. Everything may seem different, but in reality little has changed except your attitude. You will still yell at your kids, act thoughtlessly, upset yourself over petty things, make an occasional fool of yourself publicly, act inconsistently, feel victimized by parking tickets, backed-up toilets, and seemingly endless lines. Every time you make love, you won't have an orgasm. Occasionally you will covet your neighbor's goods, and you will continue to wonder if you ever will understand your mother. You never will live beyond error; every day you will demonstrate your lack of total perfection. But the absolute glory of it all, the delicious irony, is that it will be perfectly acceptable. Happiness is possible without attaining sainthood.

Bliss May Not Be Easy

Facing your deepest anxieties and dreads, as you have come to learn, does not put an end to them. Nothing ever is solved once and for all. You never will experience a time without uncertainties or second thoughts. Every solution creates new problems by presenting new choices. New problems add challenge and excitement to life. Without them our lives would be one dimensional and insipid. But from your willingness to deal with your old and new conflicts will come a growing sense of freedom and joy. As you go on learning and expanding, these feelings will occur with greater regularity, while the lapses between them will dramatically shorten. Difficulties and problems will adopt a saner, more manageable quality. Incidents that once triggered tension of hysteria now will create scarcely a ripple on your emotional pond.

Nothing Is Wasted

Change will no longer be the enemy. Every experience will become an opportunity for growth. You will actively look for the challenge, not run away from it. You will accept, even enjoy, the satisfaction that assuming responsibility for your feelings and actions brings.

A series of accidents, for instance, instead of being dismissed as a run of bad luck may cause you to pause and consider that you might be rushing headlong in the wrong direction, pushing yourself too hard, or failing to see an important point in your life. Rejection, devastating in the past, now may be a growth experience rather than the cause of emotional annihilation. When it happens without judgment of who is right or wrong, and when it is not used as an indication of your lovability quotient, learning about yourself and the choices you have becomes an exciting challenge.

Though we will still experience the temporary feelings of loss and sadness that come with being human, we will find it is *we* who ultimately reject ourselves. No longer can another's opinion of us destroy our self-esteem. Wanting to learn becomes more valuable than wanting to blame. Holding others responsible for our happiness or lack of it ceases to be rewarding. We will now want to look at our own and others' behaviors with understanding and compassion.

Love Is Secured

Fear is the common denominator in *everyone's* protective responses. As you exchange fear for love, all your relationships will change in positive ways. Once you are freed from the burden and pain of jealousy, envy, and greed, power struggles will diminish in frequency and intensity. The goal is living fully, not winning skirmishes. Intimacy will become possible because you no longer are controlled by fear. You will be willing to risk loving and being loved, sharing your deepest feelings, your secrets and mysteries, and letting others share theirs with you. You will explore each other without protection and blame as discovery becomes exhilarating.

Even pain becomes an opportunity for exploration and growth, no longer crushing your spirit but rather assuming the role of guide, ushering you toward a greater acceptance of life. Once love becomes the motivating principle in life, pain and distress assume a much less active role. Love in itself, by itself, is healing; and healing on every level becomes possible as your body responds to the energy awakened by love and humor. Self-perpetuating habits of tension, stress, resentment, and bitterness are the arch enemies of ease and health. As the mind becomes increasingly loving and positive, the body follows by becoming stronger, more vital, and more resilient. I have seen this happen even with individuals whose bodies were riddled with disease. Illness or not, as their mind and body worked in unity, they felt whole and well, some for the rest of their lives.

The more you experience yourself, the more intensely appreciative you become. My son once told me a story he had learned in school. An old Indian sat in a small clearing of a great forest with his grandchild and said, "In any direction, as far as I can see, I will find enough to keep me busy and happy to the end of my days." Boredom comes only when we are not fully present. A mind freed of the constantly intrusive chatter of anxiety has more time to enjoy the richness and wonder of its existence—the compelling warmth of a friend's laughter, the heartfelt joy in sharing a meal with loved ones, the feel of a child's tiny hand in ours. As our senses categorize thousands of different items without our conscious direction, we keenly experience the fragile beauty of a dew-covered web or the smell of burning leaves; the sound of rain on a tin roof; the warmth of a summer's wind or a lover's breath against our face. We grow in appreciation of the beauty of the human body and its infinite varieties. We are works of art. Nothing is wasted, useless, or unimportant.

Much is revealed from the past that was obscured by self-consciousness and fear. We experience a growing sense of purposefulness and direction as an integral part of life. Our creativity and insightfulness expand, and we recognize the endless possibilities that lie before us to experience beauty, satisfying work, sensual pleasure, and, above all, love. The impossible becomes increasingly possible as we open to the adventures of each new moment.

Self-Consciousness Disappears

As our confidence and sense of personal power grow, the more of ourselves we express and the easier and more natural it becomes to let go. Self-consciousness diminishes and another, broader consciousness takes its place, one that permits us to lose ourselves for a time in another person or another state of awareness. This state is one in which we become attuned to being part of a larger whole, one that extends beyond our bodies to encompass a global or universal vision. Our personal scenarios have shifted from a view of life as frequently wrong, boring, lacking, painful, and frightening to life as sometimes frustrating but always beautiful, humorous, joyous, fulfilling, touching, awesome, inspiring, and infinitely connected to each and every thing.

You'll Stay in Love

My fundamental belief is that, as human beings, we can experience only two ways of being: We live in love or in fear. In fear we remain ignorant, diseased, powerless, and unconscious of the beauty and love inherent in our true nature. To live without fear is to live in love, in harmony with ourselves and others, and to awaken to the unimagined experiences of well-being and joy that lie ahead on our journey through life. The best of what we are and the worst—all of us—is a miracle when we live in love.

Let It Be

What we most need to learn we already know.

One morning approximately two years ago, I awoke from a dream with the lines of the following poem ringing through my mind, like the lyrics of a familiar song. As I wrote them down in the quiet of that new morning, I was overwhelmed with joy, for I found within the lines a message that seemed to distill the meaning of my life.

Here in a few simple words were the bones, meat, and essence of everything I had struggled so hard and so long to learn. Since that time I have shared the poem with many friends, and now it is my pleasure to share it with you. In many ways it sums up everything I have wanted to say to you, and I offer it here with the sincere wish that you will find it, as I did, a succinct reminder of the what and why of this journey.

> Name what you feel,
> Name what you want,
> Name what you need,
> Name what you do
>   . . . and become wise.
>
>
> Quiet the judging,
> Quiet the numbing,
> Quiet the dreading,
> Quiet the punishing
>   . . . and become free.

Rest into rage,
Rest into grief,
Rest into pain,
Rest into fear

      . . . and become loving.

Let it heal you,
Let it teach you,
Let it awaken you,
Let it empower you,

      Let it be, and be transformed.